INVINCIBLE TEARS

VOL.1

TEARS YOU CAN'T SEE ONLY FROM THE MIND AND HEART.......

JULIUS CLARK JONES

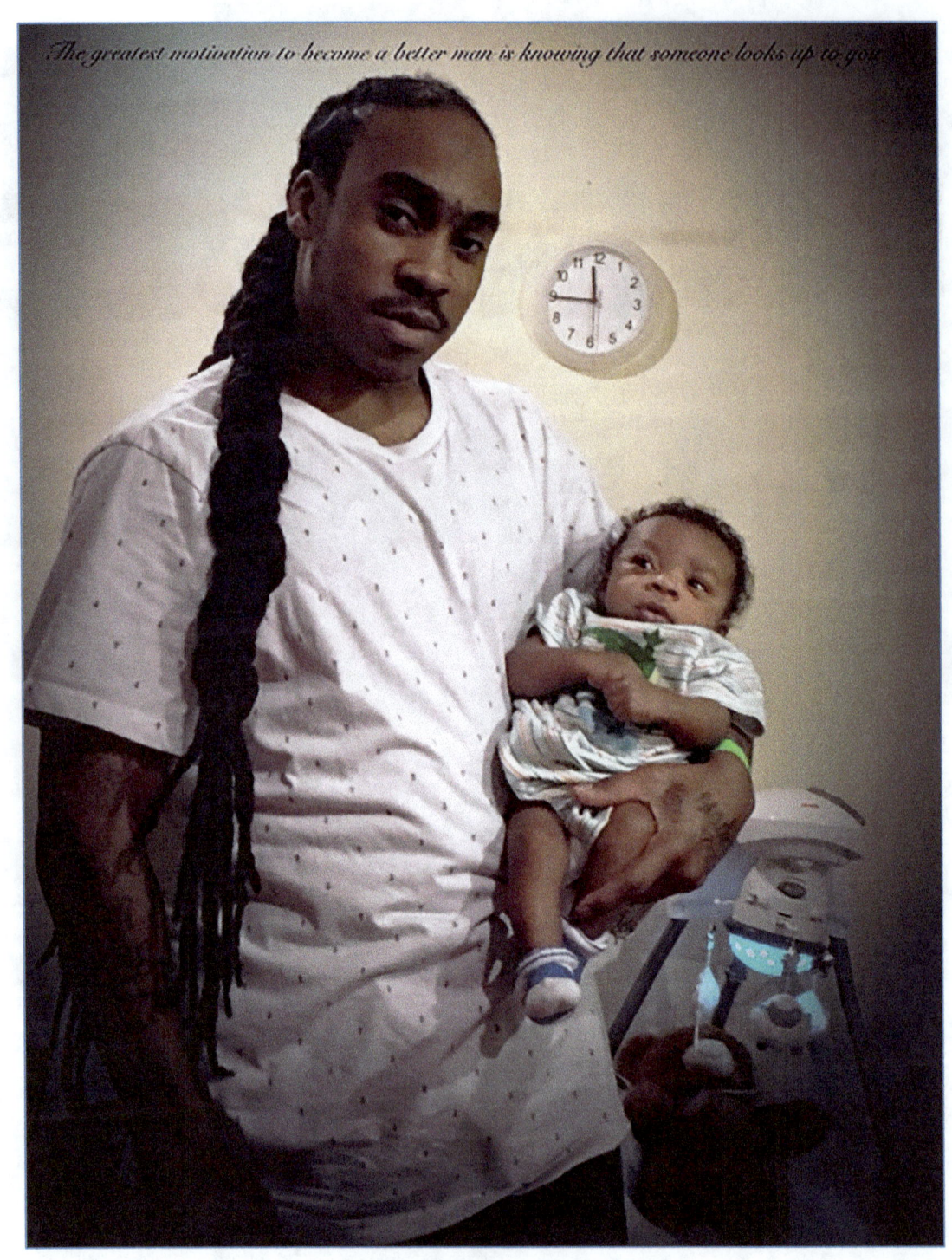

Julius Jones
Ausar Jones

Contributors

Ronnie Jones,

Uvg Trey,

Trey Boney,

Juelz,

Carolyn Hamilton,

Tephlon, Chance Sumter,

Erica Gardner,

TIFF Bonnie,

Rhonda,

Cash,

Ny'sheik,

Brenda Lewis,

HBo, Kaoss,

B G, Jabatha,

Annette Boney Kennedy,

Pappy Law,

Anthony Beckham,

Lillian Davis,

Massacre,

Twist, Big L

Emanuel Jones,

Poe,

Hollow Tip,

Deacon Charles Anthony,

Big Sha, Hard Head,

Edwin Fernandez,

rapper Jon,

Samuel Jones,

Trapper John

In Loving Memory

My Brother Tai"Quwan Boney, My Brother Samuel Jr., My Sister Lakeesha Davis,

Chuck Taylor, Y G, J Vito, Lil B G, Lady Break Bread, Spazz, Meech, Aieshia, Kim

David Q Murray, Elijha T. Murray, Yvonne and Charles Peebles, Oyg Redrum

Jalil D, Sharon Evon Murray, Antione "Twenty" Burks, Damu, Lil Steve

My Forever Queen Big Mama Joyce, I just know

That I'm making you proud....

Chapters

Introduction 7

My Godfather (Ny'Sheik) 10

Unity Became the Thang of the Past (Twist) 12

Lack of Love from My Mama (Bonnie) 16

My Mama Wanted Something More for Me (Uvg Trey) 18

The Death of My Brother (Hard Head) 19

A Message About My Brother from Another (Buck) 22

I'm Blessed to Still Be Alive (Tephlon) 24

Karma (Erica Gardner) 26

A Gangster Is a Gangster Is Not (Emanuel Jones) 27

Not Receiving Love at Home (Pappy Law) 29

This Isn't da Internet (Tweak) 31

The Feds a Wake-Up Call (Poe) 35

Felt Like a Loser Watching My Kids Grow Up Through Pictures (Julius) 37

Still Fighting My Case (Emanuel Jones) 39

The Steps I Made Becoming a Sous Chef (Cash) 41

From Being Bullied to Being Respected (Chucky Cheese) 44

Just A Little Girl (Lady Kountry) 47

Trials & Tribulations of Being Gang Raped (Lillian Davis) 52

Through It All, I Became a Healer for Young Ladies in Women (Bubbles)	59
Through Trial & Error I Stood by His Side (Juelz)	62
Becoming A Deacon Was Destiny (Charles)	64
Everything Is Not Always What It Seems (Big Sha)	67
My Family Counting on Me (Top Shelf)	68
Bloods and Crips Peace Treaty Out Harlem New York	70
Holding Accountability (Massacre)	73
Product Of My Environment (Big L)	79
Young Lost Soul (Rico)	85
It's More About Me Than Being from Piru	89
Memory of My Brother Tai	94
During Father Duties	95
My Rap His Reality	97
Not Giving Up on My Son	99
Retaliation	100
I Protected My Son	102
Way Too Young	103
Never Turn Down Nothing	104
A Line Up	105
So Called Friends	106
Being Snitched on By da Same Person Put You On	107

Introduction

My name is Julius Jones. Nice to meet everyone's acquaintance. When I was put on my set Fruit Town Brims 30's 36st. It was about camaraderie, a sense of belonging, looking for something you weren't receiving from home. 'Love'

The person that was standing right beside you was right or wrong. Way before social media, the camera was authentic; you had to be involved. Banging is about recognition and never forgetting the dead. If you came for 1 of mine, I was coming for 3 of you. There's no such thing as eye for eye in gang banging. Which led me to three consecutive cases. I beat a 25 year and 18-year sentence, yet mostly thrown out due to lack of no witnesses.

I took 11 years in the feds which I had 4 C. I's (Confidential Informants) when I was rearrested, I was informed quite a few people were happy I was locked up. That's when I knew I was completely done with the streets yet from the county to the state prison. I was always popping off or 23 in 1 in lockup.

'til the US Marshals snatched me from Northern State Prison took me to the feds. I started to unlearn and relearn to get ahead. I was tired of being tired. I wanted my queens (daughters) to be proud of me.

So, I started writing out a plan for when I get released from federal prison. You don't plan to fail; you failed to plan. Now today I'm a Credible Advocate. I do gang prevention, interventions there's educational guidance, peer mentoring, trauma and depression etc. Also, do public speaking at high schools, colleges and centers. Looking to do elementary school's reason being these kids start smelling themselves in 3rd and 4th grade. What made me come up with this concept of my book? Especially dealing with neutrals in gang members being out in the streets.

Everyone somewhat forms or fashion goes the same route. It's one thing to speak on endless issues yet it's another to actually see the work of those speaking on the issues throughout the communities. That's by actually rolling their sleeves up to make an impact within their communities. So not only speaking on streets, gangs, raped, incarceration. How some of the characters are really saving lives?

We are in a time where everything in today's society is that everything is accepted. Yet, at times I even wonder if anyone is really paying attention to what is really going on here? Does anyone even give a damn that you have major companies, continuously making in putting gang material into brand clothing. The whole music industry is selling death, the only way for you to become an artist if you are either associated with a gang.

You are a gang member yourself to promote the usual, what society already looks at us as a whole anyway. Oh, you would like to know what that is huh? Dropping out of school, selling drugs, abusing women, raping women, in and out of prison, don't take care of our kid's. Promote how we are always willing to rob, shoot and kill one another. More so over streets in blocks that we don't even own, this is how much they (The Industry) look at you. We made it comfortable as men instead of protecting our sisters, to record a situation every time a young lady is being abused.

Laughing while she's being disrespected, even beat on. What if that was your mama, what if that was your sister or niece. A relative that looked at you as a father, older brother, she never had one. There is too many pretending to be men, when in reality they are cowards. Age is nothing more than a number, you can be grown and still have a boy heart. The black woman is the most disrespected on this earth.

So, I'm here to say. I'm motivated and dedicated to having young men and men being men again. As time goes on and we grow as men, we become responsible for those who come after us. It's our job to learn and teach based on the mistakes we made on the way to manhood. We must teach our future. How not to make the mistakes we made, if not all our hard times were in vain. Also, there's a time when sacrifices need to be made in order to progress to be achieved in the future. Not every time will be looked upon as what one should do.

As a man. He will see and understand. Some sacrifices are minor, while others are major and at times even life threatening. The question is.... are we willing to make the sacrifices in how much we are willing to sacrifice for our loved ones and their future.

My Godfather (Ny'Sheik)

My uncle, Julius, so I called him but more so of a father who has been there since, I can remember. From pampers too close to pre-school and teaching me how this world goals. Not allowing me to fall victim to the negative ways of the streets but plant my 10 toes firmly on this earth with the intentions to become great and successful. Helped mold me into an achiever. When my godfather Julius went to prison these changed. As many youths that walked the path of my teenage years have been full victims of the negativity of the streets. I too fell into this day. I struggled to pick myself back up from the whole allowed myself to dig from a false sense of brotherhood.

My mother always instills in me how Julius came with clothes, shoes and is always around playing with me. Making sure I had everything I needed; she said he was a protector. No one who loves you will risk your freedom or life. My uncle never allowed that to come to me from his direction. When it continuously tried to grab ahold of me, he helped guide me to the right path. Even still now he comes through and I feel like having my godfather in my life now keeps me grounded. Knowing that, I can confide in my godfather Julius and there is no judgment, only words of advice. Makes me feel like I can humble myself, let my guard down and accept the direction from my godfather Julius. Cause I know the direction is all the right steps on the right path.

Anytime, I needed advice or to talk even if he's on his way to work he's always making time. Even now at about 1 in the morning and checking on his grandson making sure everything copacetic study on my end that's love in its for show appreciated word is born. The movement he is so passionately investing his blood, sweat and tears in. Is not just something he just started, he's been doing this for 23 years of my life and as far as I am no longer. Invincible tears aren't just an escape for troubled youth, it's a movement to save the plagues in the damaged young society we have. Just a little bit of faith and you 2 can be on the path to success and achieve your dreams. My godfather Julius is more than a figure for our generation; he's an idol for the future of the youth that we are trying to save from oppression.

Unity Became the Thang of the Past (Twist)

As a child my hobbies were everything. I played all the sports, from basketball to golf. I didn't have much growing up, so I cherish everything I read. I had a lot of dreams as a kid. One was that my pop would show up to one of my birthdays yet just never happened. Another dream of mine was to rap. I always listen to rap because of my mother. And I also had dreams of being an architect. I could draw and I love construction. Will tried to give me or started me in the streets and was honestly just trying to keep from being bored.

I didn't think that the things I was doing at a young age were bad. I just thought I was having fun. I saw all the drug dealers but I wasn't into selling drugs. It was all about fun. A lot of my friends were older so, I just hung around them and most of the time just doing that got me in trouble. Hustlers will always ask me to sell their drugs because they knew I was smart and they liked it that I had the mindset of someone older. I never sold drugs when I was young. I was too busy having fun. I got put on to my set Fruit Town Brick City Brims 232 before, I even knew I did honestly.

I grew up with the boys from my set. Knew their moms, hung out with them, ate, made money and got locked up with them before I was Brim. When I was younger, I didn't want to be a part of a gang. I knew I didn't need it and I didn't want people to ever think, I got put on for protection. But when my gram mother died, I was lost, alone, and mad. They were the only ones who cared. So, I took to be in their family Fruit Town Brick City Brim cause, I didn't have any. There was a massive structure before I was put on. Massive unity, almost as if they were a part of an army. They were militant and to me everyone could have been a twin because they all act the same.

Same aggression, same passion towards it, like I had a big brother and they all made sure I was good. Other sets at this time were out of control; only sets that still had order were 135 St West Side Piru, Queen St Bloods/ Ill town Double ii Bloods 235, Lot Boyz Bounty Hunter Bloods and 52nd St Bloodstone Villains. They all move like the family and had order opposed to the East Coast based sets, were out of order, killing each other. That was a no for us. The differences in when I was put on is that what I just said. We had more order and structure. We were more like a family. Now it has no structure. No order. Nobody couldn't be Brim when I was put on. You had to be vouched for.

Definitely face many gang-related wars. Some four serious shit and some for stupid shit that, I knew we should've been smarter about but at them times you didn't just state your opinion. If your brother rolled out then you don't say shit you just rod. Attended 2 funerals. I don't do funerals. Didn't do family funerals. Something about seeing them is that they are helpless, and can't speak to you anymore. Feel like once they die, I don't know that body in physical form anymore. Only reason I'm like that is because my whole family died before I hit 10 years old. Only people alive were 2 uncles', one aunt. My relatives, my siblings and my mother. I've never been shot but all had a gun to my forehead plenty of times and shot at. Thank God! Wasn't shot or stabbed. I believe in 10 steps ahead

People, places and things. Most definitely got feelings. If I wasn't feeling the scenery, I told my homies, I was out. A gangster told me there isn't such a thing as being scared when you're thinking smart. So, I continued to think smart and luckily it kept me away from getting shot or stabbed. I lost plenty of loved ones. Countless memories play in my head daily about the ones I lost and how they died in which. I was around to be the one to tell them it's time to go. I wouldn't want my son or relative to be put on, but the life we live is never generated. So, I'm strict on teaching my kids about the things they need to survive in real time. Not gangster time. I teach them about credit and starting their own business instead of growing up wanting to work for someone else.

I teach them everything I lack. Honestly, prison raised me. I had time to reflect on my whole childhood. The mistakes I made coming up. Because I didn't have shit or nobody being incarcerated didn't faze me. It was another school for me. I learned many lessons. Nobody ever was able to influence me negatively. And, I didn't even put myself around those types of people. I've always respected home girls and kept them as sisters. Never used them, never had sex with them, always treat them like family with respect period they were very well respected. Couldn't go anywhere without them getting us into a fight. Laughs... At this point in my life, I'm forced on many things, many goals. It's not easy with my past but it's coming along bit by bit.

I would not recommend anything about a gang to a child. It's nothing like it was. I didn't even recommend it then. A lot of hurt, memories, mental issues come with it. My message to any parent is pay attention to your child. Read the signs. Staying out late, drinking, smoking, certain video games. Music, videos, certain TV shows. Peer pressure isn't only physical now, you can get pressure just by watching TV now. Spend time with your children. Pick their brain, get to know them inside out. Take them around old friends, old neighborhoods and show them around. Then take them to nice neighborhoods and let them meet other people and show them around. I watch their reactions. Pay Attention! if you won't, somebody else will. It may not be in the best interest for them.

BRIMLETTS

Lack of Love from My Mama (Bonnie)

It started with my relative, shit with my mother it wasn't good at all. I felt she didn't love me at times. So, I started searching for love in the streets with friends etc... I actually grew up in my set 62 Harvard Park Brims. So, I knew most of everyone who was from 6214 Harvard Park Brims. I also dated a guy in my teenage years who brought me into the circle and introduced me to the banging lifestyle. At times it was fun and I took a liking to it quickly. Eventually, I took on that role as a member and not to mention his Bonnie. The first intense moment was a drive-by shooting from a rival gang which was a very scary experience as a youth. Nonetheless, I continue to hang out and be a part of the lifestyle.

Honestly it created a different person. I had no compassion for the opposite side and I hated those individuals. What made me slowdown was me losing my home boys to the streets and not to mention some disloyalty. I was always taught death before dishonor! I started observing things very differently over the years and lost a lot of homies to these streets that don't love no one. I will give young women advice and tell those individuals to go to school, college etc... Knowing what I know now. I missed out on a lot of growing up but I would not change my experience. My past is what made me the woman standing before you today!

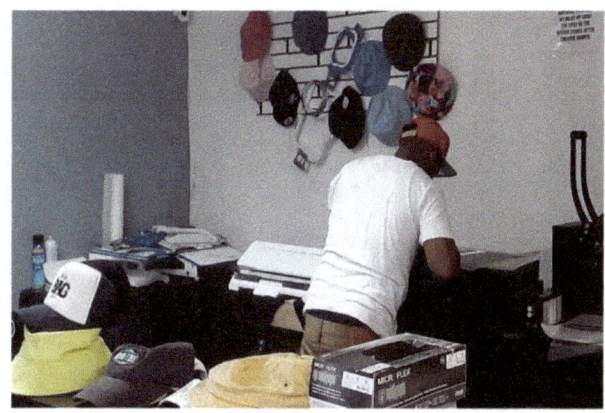
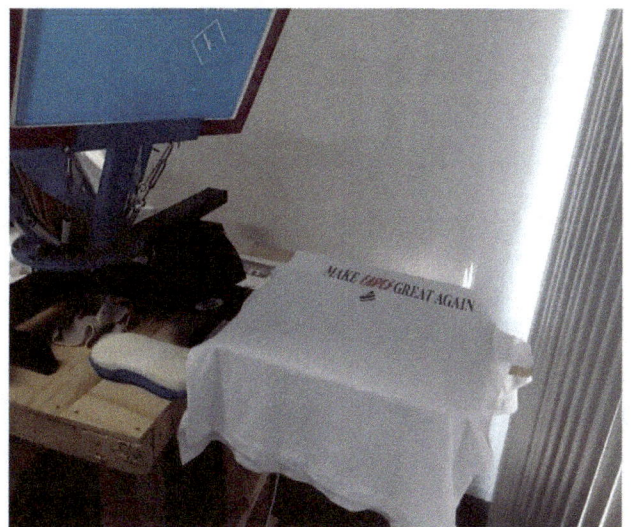

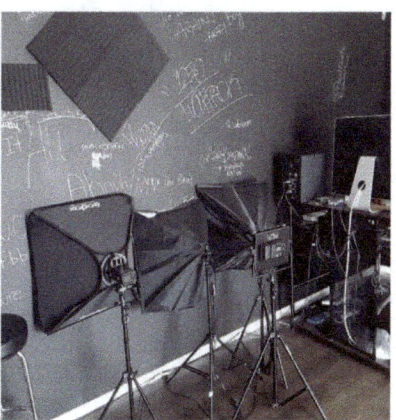

My Mama Wanted Something More for Me (Uvg Trey)

For me it was my mother even though I was born and raised in the set Fruit Town Brims 35th St. After my big relative, little KB, died who I looked up to. like a father in a big brother figure. My mother couldn't take it and knew the route I was headed so she moved to Cleveland, Ohio. It would only let me come back for the summer and never could stay any longer. Every time I came back, I came back with bad habits till she finally stopped that.

Don't get me wrong, I got into a lot of street shit in Cleveland but it was like home and I knew it was more to life than what's in Cleveland. Plus, my mom taught me responsibility very early and how to pay my own bills such as my first summer job at 14 years old. Where I had to pay her 100 dollars every two weeks for rent and buy my own clothes and shoes. And from that moment on, any money she gave me was just a loan. I had to pay it all back every time so by my 20s Cleveland ran its course so, I had to go back home to L. A. At this time, I'm not too much into the banging aspect.

The time I spent in Cleveland alone holding my own, I was just coming back to be around my family and get money. Now, I have my daughter so now, I'm driving to make it better for her when she gets older. So now I run a T-shirt printing company and I'm a journeyman carpenter by trade. My clothing brand is' 'Always Loyal '' clothing. It came about as a spin off from my record label clothing line. Then, I had problems with getting my friends to wear it for fear of attachment to the gang. So, I had to come up with something that was neutral that everyone can wear and something I'm very passionate about. My loyalty means the most to me so I came up with "Always Loyal" clothing.

The Death of My Brother (Hard Head)

Born May 6, 1988 the baby out of seven of my mother and father was raised in Flatbush, Brooklyn, NYC. I'm the identical twin's name Jacob and my twin brother is Joseph. As kids we would dress up alike and for the most part were sweet kids until 1996. One of our older brothers started banging a New York based set called N.T.G (Nine Trey Gangsters) then things changed in my life. I was nine years old at that moment and me and my twin didn't know anything much about gangs. I started to see my brother getting into fights and shootouts, selling drugs because my mother put him out. So, we didn't see my brother much unless he came to see us or pick us up from school. School wasn't a problem for us.

Our grades were excellent and we were on the" National Honor Roll" from grades 6th through 10th. Things changed in 2003 me and my twin brother's outlook on gangs, when my older brother was killed in a (gang related) shooting in Crown Heights Brooklyn. While he and I were walking to the corner store I was shot in my right leg. Me and my twin brother never really bounced back from his death; it left a big scar on us. Which led us getting put on to the set N.T.G (Nine Tray Gangster). At first, we were always together every day. We all stayed in the same hood, we bang together yet we were already taught to get down alone from our pops. We built together and fed each other but we did shootouts in robbing enemies from different hoods.

We sold drugs to stop going to school which led to us being taken from our parents and sent in a foster home. In four months, I was locked up for one year at" Rikers Island" for choking a staff member who was a Crip for disrespecting my brother. When I came home my mother was buying a house in South Carolina and was talking about getting a place in Charlotte, N.C as well. We moved to Charlotte, N.C a week later and started a new city. Finished high school and graduated. Started to learn about L.A Bloods and Crips from a documentary I saw at my uncle's house. Taught me that the jail way, I learned, was not the way to move as a member of the bloods went for two years. A Tech College got a programmer degree. I worked a few retail and construction jobs with my older brother for a couple of years then in June 2007. My oldest sister died from lung cancer; another scar left on me.

We haven't seen her in seven years. When we got back to Charlotte in 2009, I met a homie from the Fruit Town Brims set. Who brought me, my twin brother and step brother to the hood to get put on to the set. First thing I learned about Brim was" Black Revolution" and it started in L.A. So now, I am learning the L.A way of Brimin and how we started and came from about. Then in June 2010 my older brother was shot and killed at a park where he was mentoring kids at the moment, he died at the park protecting and gardening kids from the shooting. I moved back to N.Y for good while my twin brother and mother went back to N.C. So, I was alone in Brimin alone out here at first till I met 2 homies.

One in Brooklyn and one in the Bronx, what I learned from them was that I'm a man before anything else. I'm black so the odds are always against us in this system. So, in order to prove them differently, I got to do things. Does unity exist in this generation? Yes and no.... I say yes because when needed we can come together for positive energy and good vibes and laughs. At the same time, I say for the fact that unity starts with no guidance which some of these big homies have yet rather caused separation and misguided. Personal beliefs with the next young generation instead of each one teaches one.

I became a father to my first king Sebastian in 2013 as my son grows older. There are things I have to explain to him, I have tattoos, go wounds, scars from this lifestyle. I have stories he needs to know about his father and who I am. Would, I recommend my son's or any kid to become a gang member. My answer is no.

Being in a gang doesn't make you cool or anything in my opinion. You have to be born in this life or chosen. For this lifestyle of binging. Is not for the weak minded that the problem now is no structures, no leader, anybody can be a gangster. How about being a father to your kids, being a business owner, building your own clothing line. Being a role model so that your next generation learns wisdom.

Do better to want to learn about generation wealth in other business ideas. I'm currently going back to college to finish my degree in computer science. I'm planning to open a food truck in my little king's future. Oh, my savings account for school or anything they want to use it for when they are 21 my oldest having a savings of $15,000. My second has $8,000 and my newborn has $1,400. My boys will be business owners and their own interpreters and they have me to teach "Business Management". My direct message to mothers that have kids is pay attention to your kids. The world you used to know is gone; it's a new age, a new generation. Is not going to be easy, talk to the kids about everything, the pros and the cons of this lifestyle. Everything isn't as glorious as it seemed on the Internet or TV. This way a life can led you to prison or be killed following a dangerous path.

A Message About My Brother from Another (Buck)

Ever since the day I met Julius he has always been a firm individual. Always being confident enough to stand on any choice that he was willing to make. Julius and I were like night and day but we respect each other's good traits and force on making each other the best version of ourselves. Of course, we disagree with each other but we knew it was with the best intentions. Julius is like a brother to me which he then turned around and became an uncle figure to my kids. Julius loves my kids as if they shared the same blood. He would always ask about them and even if I wasn't around, he would see them on his own. He would continue his own personal bond with them.

Knowing the outside "streets" were dangerous, "Julius" knew and made sure to lead the kids away from false glamorous lifestyles; the streets betrayed whether it was four males or females. When Julius was released from prison, he turned to the youth and schools who needed guidance from someone who could tell them first-hand about the path they simply wanted to go down. I was very proud to see him in person go back to the high school we attended "Henry Snyder". He gave sound truthful advice to the youth and once again Julius didn't hold back. He talked to them in their language which he knew he had to be direct, not traditional advice.

He somehow knew that your basic standard advice only went in one ear of today's kid and out the other, so he was very direct and words he used. When you heard it, you felt the pain in love in the advice he was giving.

I'm Blessed to Still Be Alive
(Tephlon)

I was raised by as Muslim father (NOI) In Baptist mother (Church). Struggle in the home was real, being that my parents were never a couple. My siblings were in foster homes till I was like three years of age. Being the youngest out of three siblings at the time. Doing our best to make ends meet. They collect scrap metal cans and make store runs for pocket money. Started writing poetry before I wrote rhymes. At the age of 11(85-86). Got my first real job selling candy in a number house around 12 years of age, making $200 a week. Due to the almost everyday abuse in the house by my stepfather, I rebelled and ran the streets in 90-91.

The difference is from being neutral and part of a gang is simple. Your life is not as much in danger. Being neutral is a person who can vibe with any organization as long as they are not partaking in that organization's lifestyle. Being a part of a gang is a lifestyle. With very harsh consequences. What made me get put on? Nothing made me, I was thinking, I was the toughest person on earth at first. Seeking attention looking for someone to care about me. However, when you realize it's a family within a family you start to understand there is purpose in life. I needed discipline in order.

Fighting 3/4 dudes or more at one time is very much a death sentence. Your toughness will show so we wonder why everyone says why we're acting tough. If it's not in you. No need to act like it. Getting put on is not an option for some. I wouldn't encourage getting put on at all nowadays. Not the best decision in your life. If you'd never been a part of struggles of being poor, homeless and hungry in an oppressed country. No need to get put on. You have nothing in common with gang culture. Your PS4 controller is broken.

Definitely not a reasonable initiation, two years in jail, 2 years in the county prison, 7 years upstate. I felt like a slave. Then I got to understand that it is not cool being around the same folks who do the same crimes over and over. That's not a part of growth! Is a destruction prison not your friend. You're basically on the combat field and don't even know it. You can die in prison as well. I accomplished my damn lesson. I utilized it the best way without making my time more lethal. I accomplished freedom. Do the crime, do the time. I wasted some of my family's life as well.

Because, I didn't realize the impact that it had on other members in my family. No, my life will never be a waste as long as I'm alive. I have children to raise and lives to save. I'm a sous chef thanks to the art institution of Philadelphia. I have a nonprofit organization LLC. We are feeding the homeless, taking the children on trips and teaching them about working together in accomplishing things. I'm a rap artist that goes by the name Tephlon. My music streams on many platforms, YouTube, Sound Cloud, IG and many more. I'm a homeowner. I'm currently looking to invest into the food truck or restaurants industry. I sell clothes and creations to your appeal called Majestic Creations.

The message is this from the heart. Stop looking up to those guys. They are not a part of God's work. Very few will survive this error of rap 2 record deals before I went to prison. I think God said no, I have other plans. The music business wants you to do things very much out of your character. If you do, look up to these rappers. We already know that you're not in the learning stages of life. Believe me the bigger you ball the harder you fall. They have no soul! so they won't even spit on you if you are on fire. These rappers are broke. Once they want you out. It's over. Or you just got to be overtaken like a soldier because they are telling the youth to do things they won't do. They talk about killing people, and are dressed up like Prince and Michael Jackson. Look up to the people who actually help you succeed.

Karma (Erica Gardner)

As far as trials and tribulations they were many, but they were dear. You have to remember; I was born into the culture Nine Deuce Bishops Bloods to be exact. I didn't choose it, it chose me. As far as going to public schools that was a challenge in the beginning. But I've always been the bully type so that didn't bother me too much. I began to see things differently when my son got shot. He almost died because he wanted to be just like his mother.

To have to watch my son, with 11 bullets in his body, did something to me. It showed me that the lifestyle took no prisoners. I had to accept that tap on the chin and go on with life as usual. I had to deal with what countless mothers before me dealt with but my son lived. Sometimes, I feel like I live with this problem he has now as a lifelong message to me. My karma sat him there. And of course, I wouldn't recommend it to any girl or boy. The rules have changed and your own homie will be the one to put a nail in your coffin. Is about money and righteousness now. All that banging shit is for the birds.

A Gangster Is a Gangster Is Not (Emanuel Jones)

In recent days, I had a discussion with some comrades on what a gangster is. To my surprise many don't even know what a gangster is but will be the first to claim they are a gangster. Some do not know who they are, and they don't even know who they are pretending to be, which shows you just how lost many in our society are. Many have the meaning of gangster confused from watching too many movies, listening to too much gangster rap. In other mainstream media outlets. First and foremost, a gangster is a man of God, one who is unwilling to submit to the unrighteous conditions in laws that oppress him and those he loves. Gangsters are gentlemen, respectful, loyal and honorable. Gangsters are about unity, family and care.

Most people might not agree with these qualities of being a gangster because of the actions that many display in the name of a gangster. But any real gangster knows there are not too many who are really gangsters. What we call those who lack this understanding or pretenders, fakes, clowns, weak. Faking will never deliver respect. Pretending will put you in a situation you cannot handle, and if the pressure is too much for you, you won't be able to handle it. Be who you are. A gangster won't bend. A perpetrator will.

Many aspire to be gangsters for the perceived glory that comes with being such, yet they don't want to accept the responsibilities of being a gangster. Martin Luther King Jr. was a gangster. Malcolm X and Noble Drew Ali were gangsters. The Black Panthers and all unknowns who died for their rights in the struggle for equality were gangsters. Moses from the bible was a gangster. Harriet Tubman and Marcus Garvey were gangsters. Only when we commit unlawful acts for justice does it become righteous. So, what is your cause? Gators are revolutionaries, uplifting their people and dying if necessary. True gangsters are educated leaders in science, religion, medicine, politics, civil and human rights, business and social justice.

A gangster is not about having the most murders or murdering someone just because you are angry and cannot control your emotions. A gangster does not have children and abandons them. A gangster does not run from responsibility. A gangster honors his commitments. A gangster accepts his wrongs. No matter what. A gangster definitely does not take advantage of, manipulate, and exploit the minds of young men and have them kill each other for selfish benefits. A gangster never brags about their acts, whether right or wrong. If one chooses to call themselves a gangster, I hope they understand the meaning of gangster. Live with mortality in principle.

Not Receiving Love at Home
(Pappy Law)

Cassandra "Pappy Law" Hart, was born in 1971 and raised in East L.A raised in Aliso Village, home of the 1st East Coast Crips and Aliso Village Brims. Growing up in a violent community in an abusive home treated as the black sheep mother was single and I'm the baby of seven children made me accustomed to the street. My momma did her own thing and gave us freedom at age 6. In a lack of love and protection from home. Made me feel loved by the gang bangers and how they treated me, protected me and had my back better than my own family.

So, as I became more street, I began to hang with gang members because to me, I felt safe with them. I was always a kind hearted person who didn't participate in the violence that others did, I fought all the time at school or in the projects. Well basically wherever, I went. The battles that I faced going and coming from school were verbal abuse from girls, boys, fights, detention and suspension with kick outs. No, I wasn't born in the Outlaws but was particularly raised since birth. I started claiming Outlaw 20's Bloods before I got put on.

No other hoods treated me right nor had my back, especially not being born in their area or having a family that's of their set. It was the love and respect that they gave and showed me that made me say, I'm rolling with them. I've got treated based on how I carried myself. When I lost my homeboy, it broke my heart and made me bang harder. I felt like everyone was against me. Age 18, I started going to county jail and as I got older, I hit the penitentiary at 21 and did 2 1/2 years. Realize that's not my life, a lot of bad things happen to women there.

It was not fun or cool to be doing time. As a single mother my hardest trail was keeping a roof over my son's head and teaching him how to be a man every step of the way. The only assistance I got from my hood was a place to hang out, a little sleep and pushing dope for certain homies and I was able to call on a few ifs, I needed to. As a grown woman, mother, grandmother, sister and aunty in adulthood, I see that the lifestyle was a waste of time and senseless deaths.

That brought much heartache! No, I would not introduce anyone to this lifestyle and as far as following my footsteps would not be an easy or safe way of living. Honestly, I don't have any feelings towards other home girls pushing Bloods back South or the East Coast. I really don't know them but I welcome them with open arms. The message that I have for young women is don't choose this life and do your best to not bring them around that lifestyle and keep them sheltered and active in sports.

This Isn't da Internet (Tweak)

As a young in, I ended up being drawn to the streets for a couple of reasons. I was in the 7th grade. A lot of my homeboys had a lot of issues at home or just seeing things going on in our neighborhood that made us want to stick together in form our own family, watch over each other and protect each other by any means necessary. Plus, a lot of older homies from our area always stood out to me in my pops heavily in the streets so you know as a kid you can be easily influenced. When I got put on Fruit Town Brims 36st, I was looking for a solid brotherhood.

Live life, in love and protect each other. I was always big on being family oriented. When I was coming up, a lot of young homies in my age bracket were repping blocks and projects. A lot of the older homies from our hoods were already banging Bloods in Crips. We didn't gravitate to that until the ages 14-16. I was repping my block in running the streets since I was 12 but I didn't start banging Fruit Town Brims till I was 16. I lost a lot of friends to gang violence and a few relatives. The one that stuck out to me the most was when my relative Tylip was murdered. Just the way it went down just sickens me to this day.

It's disgusting the way people play with gang culture. Especially where comma I'm currently at VA. From the streets to the penitentiary a lot of dudes look at this as a fad. It's just something to do until something else comes along for them. Nobody seems to understand what they are getting themselves into until shit hits the fan. I mean when it comes to the entertainment, industry making money off our lifestyle, it's fucked up they pick whoever has the best gimmick. The appearance, the sound. They invest a bunch of money into you knowing they will eventually get back double or triple what they put out.

If you happen to be one of the dudes that was really in the streets and get caught up in some street shit which might result in prison or death, they're on to the next. They make money off our pain in everyday struggles. We don't make it any better; at the same token we give them what they want to get what we want. So, it's kind of tit for tat. It's a dirty game. I ended up in prison over a man trying to call me out over social media and disrespecting my walk of life. All for trying to impress a female in his homies. Due to the get or be got mentality, a developed over the years from my past experience in the street resulted in me being in prison with a 20-year sentence for hot one.

As far as the gang culture in prison for the ones just claiming, they eventually get their card pulled. You got some spots where some members will slide it under the rug for their own personal gain, you got some that have 0 tolerance and really live by what they signed up for and will regulate the situation however they see fit. Out here you got along with gang members, not a lot of gang bangers. I've been a part of the gang culture since 2005. I've seen a lot of people from my city lose their life before they graduated or even had their first kid. I'm 29 years old and the father of three. I'm blessed to still be here. Never seen myself living past 18. I never want to experience the feeling of losing my child to gang violence.

I've witnessed mothers when they first heard the news of their son being killed. Trust me, it's not a good site or feeling. So, I would never want my sons or my daughter indulging in that. I want them to be 10 times better people, I want them to do well in school, graduate a career and eventually have a family. I don't want them to ever feel like they need to carry the torch as far as being in the street. There's never any good and then to it it's a gamble. Some slide and make it under, some don't, some content with being just that until they leave. Also, I realize that the more years go by the grimier the game gets.

All morals, respect and principles are out the window. So, for anybody reading this, stay out on the streets. I got in touch with Julius through a homeboy of mine. It was a special occasion out of Newport News, VA. You know Julius was fresh out of the feds so he wasn't really familiar with us. We were kids when Julius went to prison. A homie from Fruit Town Brims 30's told Julius about me, saying I was from Jersey City and I was currently incarcerated. Julius asks for my information. Julius checked with another young homie from around our way to know exactly who I was and gave me his number.

Thang about it is, I already knew who Julius was since I was a little kid in that he just came home. Growing up Julius and his brother Emanuel names wrung bells around and around my way. Not to mention Julius used to run with my older relative wrong B.I.P back in the day. I remember calling Julius about how our first conversation went. For the past five years Julius has been somewhat of a mentor to me. Julius is the epitome of what a real Big Brother should be. Instead of convincing me to indulge in a bunch of gang activity while I'm incarcerated or once I'm released.

We have talked about me educating myself more, getting trades, reading more just to keep my mental sharp in just staying out the way. So, I can get back home to my family. When I hear things like Julius going to colleges, high schools, speaking on gang life, prison life and just being a black man in America keeps hope for not only just me, for my 3 kids they're coming up. Not to mention how becoming a counselor at a local high school gives me motivation that Julius stays in contact with a lot of other brothers in prison. He stays in touch with and does the same for them. So, my love and respect for Julius will and always remain at an all-time high

The Feds a Wake-Up Call (Poe)

When I was young, around 10 to 15 years of age. My hobbies were drawing. I love every single thing about art and creativity. I wanted to be an architect growing up. Not many people where I come from were given the opportunity to achieve their dreams. At least that's what, I thought. Property was all around. There was no escaping it. Everywhere you looked at the dealers on the corner made it look really easy to change all that. Being an architect became an afterthought once; I was introduced to the streets. It all came so naturally.

Besides that, it was my neighborhood. Why shouldn't I benefit from it like older guys do? Becoming an architect requires too much work. You had to get very familiar with different math and arithmetic. It was easier to count money. Once 2005 rolled in, I was introduced to another culture that pledged our community, killing off our people. Gang culture. I grew up in an era where we would represent our set Beven Nine Three Gang to the fullest. One on One fist fights to all out brawls with other sets. So, when the colors came in to play it was only natural that me and many others fell victim to the gang culture.

It didn't take long for what started as something strong and beautiful to turn into something dishonest. At the beginning, everything was love. I mean every set displayed their honor for this B Thang. Weren't too many wars until numbers were acquired. It seemed as if the more people joined each gang the more cats were tripping on other homies to prove dominance. Many good homies lost their lives to the death and prisons over a lifestyle that was intended to uplift. So much division. There was no more unity amongst men at a point in time. A state of confusion. It wasn't until I caught my federal beef in "09" that caused me to wake up.

It opened my eyes to the deception of the culture. It made me see that every soldier didn't honor the rules and regulations we all took upon the life we led. That, along with meeting legendary men of the underworld who had movies made based on their lifestyles, were. The eye opener for my big brother (the person who introduced me to the culture). The one person I knew whose whole heart was into this Damu thang even had a change of heart. Right there and then, I knew that the game had changed. Playing field was stacked against us. What I do today is be a father, a family man. Started my own business T & G Grounds Keeping LLC.

Felt Like a Loser Watching My Kids Grow Up Through Pictures (Julius)

Me watching my youngest daughter grow up, not only through pictures, take her first steps at visit, speak of first words at visit. My youngest Zy'onna helped guide me to be motivated in something greater. Locked in at "Northern State Prison" the day my middle daughter at the age of two years old laid across my lap. Lock eyes with me seeing how much she wants to need me home. After the visit was over, I just went straight to my cell and kept replaying the same image over in my head of how her face looked when she said it.

Just stared out the window while the tears fell from my eyes, I'm in prison holding up the set, pressing a hard long. My 2-year-old just told me how she was hurting. I watch her take her first steps through a glass window. That doesn't make me know man, nothing real about it. Us as young men and men have to make better choices in decisions. Remember being at 595 Newark Ave Jersey City, New Jersey, the big courthouse. That day Fruit Town Brims were thick and most had the same charges. Hot ones, attempted murders or a shooting with a gun possession.

Me going inside the courtroom, seeing my oldest face wash all my worries. I still didn't realize how being locked up in her seeing me and chains affected her, my oldest my Princess. She broke down at the courthouse when the judge said next time, he saw my face and he was gone, give me life. He's going to make sure of it, he's tired of seeing my face. She was crying so much, the judge recommended, I get 20 minutes with my daughter in the conference room. The path we take in life not only affects you, any of us that's running

 around these streets, those close to us change the cycle. My oldest daughter Princess taught me love.

So, what would it take before you realize? Your babies value your presence more than money. In all reality let's be honest it's not even about feeding your babies. Do they have their own bank accounts, just in case something happened to you? Money for college, trade school put away? They long for materialism and at the moment countless think that it's wonderful they kid in the hottest gear. Yet they lack the means to teach their kids about surviving, responsibilities and putting their needs before wants. Chasing meaningless dollars is going to have you miss them being born, first words, steps. Our kids daily or being left behind feeding for themselves yet countless think our kids don't have the right to be upset.

I went away when my oldest was five years old and touched down when she was 16. Even though my cases had nothing to do with drugs. Chasing the very dollar have you out there in the very first place gets caught up in everything else. Even though it's been over seven years, I can't get back that time. I refuse to put a dollar sign before my goddess when it's not beneficial. If I can work for cents in the prison then, I can work for any amount in the world. My goddess is priceless.

Still Fighting My Case (Emanuel Jones)

My case was in the state first, never being offered any plea agreements because they never had a case. Until the so-called homie took a deal, turned around and snitched even still nobody took a deal. The system wanted me so bad they pushed the case to the feds. It is when they started tying other bloods into my case. I didn't even know. They started making up stories and snitching on whomever just to get out whatever situation they had going on. Everyone that snitch was from Fruit Town Brims or Brick City Brims that they betrayed to love.

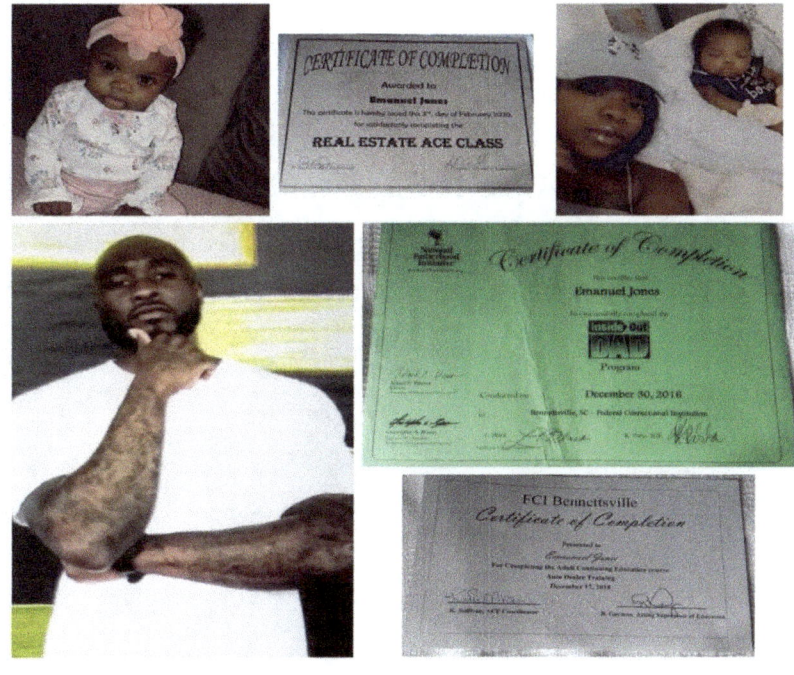

I'm still fighting because someone admitted in court from day one. I had no involvement and he admitted it in court he did it, let alone sign after Davis. He even got caught with the murder weapon. I have watched my only daughter grow up through pictures from a little girl, to now a grown young lady. Now having her own daughter. I have over 17 years on a 30-year bid. While I'm in prison, I spend most of my time knowing myself better, understanding the conditions that got me here. Accepting the fact, I never want to come back to prison if I must change. My thought process in those around me.

I've realized mostly what got us here is the pain we endured that led us to the wrong choices. Being in the streets and getting caught up in the criminal atmosphere and being guilty by association. So, I studied from the day I was incarcerated until this day to gain knowledge and wisdom of not only myself but others also. To learn more about business and teach the youth what I learned so they will have a chance when they are free to succeed and stay on the streets. I gained many certificates in financial literacy, real estate, business management, culinary arts, economics, and the fundamentals of communication.

I gave speeches to prisons about self-awareness, taught classes of spirituality. I counsel youth and help people build credit and teach business skills. I turned my time in prison as an opportunity to educate myself further even when they couldn't let me take college courses. I had too much time. I bought test books and taught myself. Invincible Tears represents all those in poverty going through the struggle of survival to sustain the economic conditions to help feed their family. We all have dread tears coming down our face from the hurt and pain we experience just trying to live a normal life growing less fortunate.

I want to help erase their tears from our youth and help guide them to make better choices. Give them an outlet to speak to those who can relate to them when they don't feel comfortable speaking with their parents. Help them make choices that will stop the cycle of continued poverty and guide them to financial freedom.

The Steps I Made Becoming a Sous Chef (Cash)

I grew up in Jersey City, New Jersey. My mother's side of the family are from the projects downtown Jersey City. My dad was from Jersey City (Bramhall to be exact). I would say, I was raised well. My mom worked hard every day and she did her best. She couldn't do everything; she was still human. My pops weren't a stay at home take you to the park dad my father was heavily in the field but he always worked too. He was completely against the government and honestly really didn't like white people.

I grew up happy and angry but angrier from seeing things my mom went through and always wanted my pops. I knew I was going to my grandma; I saw my dad so, I always went. My dad was my first idol as a kid because I didn't see him as much as I wanted to so my interest was really high. Don't get me wrong my dad was around just not like I wanted him to be. I don't blame him. I had to grow up and become a man and learn you can't teach what you haven't been taught. Fast forward, I had an out of nowhere interest in football.

My mom signed me up and as time went by, I wanted to be just like Emmitt Smith the running back for Dallas cowboys he broke the record for running backs with only one arm he made choice it was then I knew that's the strength I want not just in football but in life. My pops made it to 2 games my whole football career my mom slowed down my senior because she was busy and didn't have the time. I went to college played for a bit but football was over and I couldn't see it. When I finally could I lost all idols, nobody could speak to me I wasn't distracted by something I loved anymore there was nothing I loved. So, I went back to my pops he was getting money I wanted money. He was a known street person. He was known to be vicious I wanted to be vicious because that was all I knew of him is stories like that nobody told me he went to school or did those good things because everybody in this world is to judge mental of the next person. So, I stepped off the porch at 19 and got active.

Time went by I got my friends and we did our thang. Fast forward to I'm about 24 -25 I felt like a man and I was ready for a man shit I started hanging with my cousins they asked me" what you know about Fruit Town Brim" I said I only know what the city show niggas ratting niggas wanting to be bigger than the set and making selfish decisions that hurt everybody and make certain G homies who made real sacrifice live in vain. I started to meet good people solid people that I knew wasn't faking so I got out on the set it wasn't no passes it wasn't no brakes and before that moment I was angry from feeling alone I lost love in myself now I had a family of some niggas who felt and thought just like me.

I always took the illegal chances, I always made decisions that was either win or lose no in between. I started losing homies to prison or the graves started to see it was a one-way Street and the only way to continue that is to not live myself nor the people who genuinely love me. I knew, I had talent but always ignored or felt, I had something to prove. I met a teacher who got me to see certain things and realize how trick we all was. Doing the system job for them by getting us to hate ourselves and each other next.

What was really the eye-opener for me was once I started seeing certain homies idolized and wanted to be just like becoming football coaches, family men, youth influence, speakers it was then I started to realize what real gangster was.

My whole college career came, I had 14 warrants and eight different cities. I was literally sneaking to school. I finally got my life in order and now graduated in May of 2021 before getting a degree in "Culinary Arts" and I'm good at it too. I couldn't see my life past today in that same drive-in determination. I went into the streets. I re-direct the same energy towards my passion for goals. Then, I met Julius" the "Author. The first thing he said to me was to read a book on the history of blacks. I never said "Julius' ' but I read the book he sent me in that book made me stand as man. I'll never turn my back on the set. I never lose my edge, I always tap in.

I always check my homies and offer help if I can. I had a teacher who made me evolve better for my family one last time. I knew I had a talent and it was time to use them. That teacher was Julius "The Author" and I can't thank you enough.

From Being Bullied to Being Respected (Chucky Cheese)

I was born Charles Leston Pebbles. I was born in Belize City in Central America on February 20th 1969. I was six years old when my parents sent for me and my two sisters to go to Los Angeles, California. My first place we lived was on thirty ninth and Dalton. Which was a Crip Neighborhood but I was into that. I like playing American football, for the first four or five years.

Then we moved to 36th Place between Budlong and Catalina. That's when I met the homies Big KB, G Dogg, Boola, Batchy, Pockets and a few more. I started hanging with the homies from about 1981. Once, I started hanging with the homies. It all started for me. I used to go to Catholic School Holy Cross 7th grade 1981. Me and my older sister but as the days went by the more, I got into the streets. I started to bang from day one, I didn't know it but I was involved.

I started to have a lot of fights with the homies just because I was from a different country. I used to be teased for being from Belize but I stood my ground. The homies started to embrace me once, I started to put it down and I was small and skinny. So, I had a chip on my shoulder too. So, I found myself a part of the Fruit Town Brims 36th Streeter. I live on 36 place 1225 but everybody hangs on 36 St by the homie Danny Ray house. But this is how I got my name. The homie Moe used to clown me and say I look like Dat at the pizza spot Chuck E Cheese.

At first, I didn't like it. I like the name B Boy but everyone just kept calling me Chuck E Cheese or Chucky. I love my name because I made it known. LOL We'll continue my life in the hood world starting Drinking, Smoking Weed, Cigarettes Newport. Also, I thought I would be a gang banger, I was going to do my part. So, I dressed the part and just started busting my gun fighting with Crip niggas gunning Crips down. This is the 80s. 84-85 was my best years but the only thing is I stayed going in and out of jail.

I went to jail in 1986 for a year, got out and continued with the same shit but I started to rob jewelry stores. I had a crew; I used to deal with it but after a while. I was getting older and I had a girl so I moved out of the hood like it was 1988. We went out to the valley to sell dope to my other crew. This was more drugs dealing with homies. After little A Dog died, we went to the Valley then some more homies came out that way. There were a lot of Crips out there from different hoods but at home he told us we weren't out here for that. We're here to check money but it was enough for everyone to eat. But I kept getting into it with niggas out that way.

I just hold the heat and bust when needed...lol I had my son in March of 1990 and my daughter in May of 1990. So yeah, I had my girl in my side chick having my baby at the same time fucked up situation at that time. And once again in 1991, I went to a party in Inglewood where, I got into it with these niggas so, I pull out my gun and let loose. I got caught up again. Police came to my apartment where; I was staying. Tarzana gave me five years and got out 1994 April. Got out with the fuck the world mentality five months later, got caught up again. Got into it with these Crips they bust and I bust back. Police came got me to come in, one thing I will always and never forget.

When my mother pulled up, when they had me and those police cars. She just stood there and looked at me and looked down, I was hurt because I knew she was hurt. Oct 1st 1994 to February 5th 2013 eighteen years and four months later, I got deported back to Belize. Six months later, I got caught with a gun they gave me five years ago. There for years but I'm tired. I'm done, I'm done then I lost everything my mom died when I was in prison 2008. My dad died in 2013 when I was here. Only have my two sisters and my kids. But I haven't seen them since 1994. I talk to them on the phone but in 30 years, I haven't seen them. I love them and they love me....

Just A Little Girl (Lady Kountry)

John McNeil Junior High: 1968

Before Junior High:

Last day of school in elementary no more 61st street Elementary School, my twin and I were moving on up to Junior High, the 7th grade. We were going to John Muir Jr. High School on Vermont Ave. We graduated from the school auditorium, and later were allowed to have a graduation party at the house. We dance with our 6th grade Elementary friends until about 7:00 PM. Big sister Lashawne talked mom into letting my twin and I go to a night party. Mama trusted Lashawne; she was already in my thoughts into life since six grade.

I used to spy on her and thought she was doing some cool shit. Smoking, cutting class and sometimes, I would see her other six graders from 61st street Elementary in the tunnel. Smoke would be coming out of the tunnel on 61st and Grand like it was a fire. Hopefully the tunnel is closed up now, due to a few dead bodies found in them over the years. And of course, Broadway was two blocks away from Grand and some areas were the whole stroll in the 1960s. Also, I will sometimes see girls hopping cars with men.

Later, I found out those men were " Trick", So yeah, my sister Fonz started early too. We got to the party and these were older kids, maybe 10th graders and up. They were partying, music blaring, some were dancing, some standing around alone or in groups shooting the jive puffing on cigarettes. I love to dance and that's what I did. I had no problem keeping the dance partner or I would dance alone. Around midnight we had to be back home and Lashawne took us home. She had one of her friends. It might have been Denise Tannen who was found dead a few years later in one of the tunnels on 68th and Grand.

When we got home, I was naturally amped up. I really had a great time at the party with the older young people. While coming up, mama was always partying with her family or deaf friends at our house or at one of the relatives, but we were not allowed in those parties. Kids stay in their place, so it was truly freeing to be a part of older people even by a few years. Lashawne talks Mom into letting us go to an afterhours party. This party started around mid-night till the wee hours of the morning.

I don't remember what time my twin and I and sister Lashawne got home, but I do remember this party was on 54th off of Hoover, not too far from home, as we lived off of Bonsallo and Hoover nice house and they were playing the long version of running away child. Well of course, I immediately got on the dance floor and Belinda, my twin, sort of backed up in a corner. She was timed in a way. These were a different crowd although a few from the last party were there. That's how I was on the floor getting down so fast because one of the guys from the last party was present.

I work my groove on that song, my young budding body swaying and bogging down. The song is a good seven minutes long. As I danced, I could feel my body loosening up. I didn't know anything about marijuana but I could hear Lashawne and others saying she got the contact, while laughing. I didn't know what the contact was but I felt good. I dance the night away with grownups. Later I found out some of those people were in their 20's doing drugs, popping pills, drinking and popping acid. It was too late though. That night on a dance floor was as if I found my calling on a summer morning and I mean the wee hours of the morning and I wanted more.

I didn't know that one night was going to turn my whole life around. That summer of 1968, started off as one night in June and that was it for a while. Mama wouldn't let us go anywhere else, except to the oldest sister's house and Harvard Park, occasionally to swim. At my oldest sister Maureen's, we could smoke on our little cool cigarettes and play music and dance. We weren't into company when our 61st St friends went about their lives. A few we saw who lived in the neighborhood between Hoover and Figueroa, from 54th and up to Gage.

The furthest we went was to 68th in Vermont to older sister Maureen and Aunt Mary who lived off of 75th and Vermont. We were sometimes able to walk a big mama off of 74th and McKinley. We also had a few Elementary friends we would visit. The Perry girls on 58th between Hoover and Figueroa in Ellen Bradley rest in peace who live on the next block from us on Bonsallo. The people who lived off the 54th Figueroa. Sometimes we played with owl head Lewis and stopped at Pamela Williams house but not much because they were squares.

I liked them a lot but I was looking for excitement. Like the time I was about 11 and it was a Saturday night and my twin was home alone. We saw flashing lights in front of the house and there had to be the police. We peeked out the window, police were all over Bonsallo, guns drawn in waiting. I could hear someone on a bullhorn. Put the gun Down and lay on the ground. A shot rang out. Now I'm excited, and I want to see more. Me and my twin go out on the front porch but can't see anything but what's in front of the house because of the tall bush that surrounded our house.

I could see the flashing red, blue lights and cops in front of the yard in the yard on either side of the house and across the street. Our house is in the back and it's nothing but a yard headed towards the street. As I told my twin. I'm going to look, I get down on my knees and she says, I know you're not going up there! I said, I'll be back. She said Brenda as I began to crawl to the front of the yard. All around the house like in a monopoly game, with the railroads there was an opening where you could crawl through to get in or out of the bushes. Small enough for a child or 12-year-old.

I made it. I look both ways and I see police cars all up and down Bonsallo and Mr. Law from across the street standing on his porch with a gun in his hand. Oh lord, Mr. Law must have gotten drunk at the cozy corner again on the corner of 59th in Hoover. He became very mean and abusive and other than that he was alright. He would fight the lady he lives with, but her kids settled him down. Not tonight. Mr. Lou took it one step further; he picked up a rifle or shotgun and was firing it too. I was scared but I couldn't. My head swung left to right and I looked back at the house to check on my twin. Mostly the police were asking Mr. Lou to drop the weapon in surrender. Mr. Lou had been in the war.

He looked like an older man but probably wasn't. Alcohol had gotten to him. After a while, Mr. Lou surrendered and he was taken into custody. We didn't see him for a while. The next time this happens; I don't think Mr. Lou was so lucky but I will have to do research on this. I was there but I was getting high at that time. But I remember crawling up to the front of the yard again. Twin and I walked to the oldest sister's house a lot because she worked in a nursing home. Therefore, we babysit our niece and nephew. I started filling out in all the right places as I'm smelling myself. Mama worked herself so she didn't know Lashawne had passed down some of her mini dresses to us.

One day while walking to my sister's house on the 68th off of Vermont we passed this photo shop in a man walk. (I won't put his name on here, and might embarrass his family, however his mother lived on our street) and ask if we wanted our picture taken. I was really looking cute and felt good about myself. Belin my twin said no and I said yes, is it free? The man said yes. He knew us and we knew his mother. I was eleven and he may have been 35. He looked old. Twin wouldn't come in and as I looked at her looking all sad and shit.

I went in boldly; I already have pretty legs and I felt cute. That was my second time wearing that dress and after that day, it was my last time. He told me to have a seat and it wouldn't take long. I sat in the chair in a pose and he walked over and said no this is what I want you to do. His hands slid under my dress and then he touched my breasts. Ugg, I think that's why I hated old men for a long time. I felt dirty and now I hated the dress I was wearing; he made it dirty and now I was shaking up and too frightened to holla or run. He took a picture of me and told me don't say anything to anybody because no one will believe me.

I came out quietly, saying nothing and the twin asked to see the picture. A passed it to her, she said it was pretty and gave it back and I tore up the picture. Twin looked at me with her mouth open but saw the look on my face and we kept walking. We only had four blocks to go to get to my sister's house. I was tainted. I currently couldn't erase that away with cigarettes, but I said nothing. I had only that weed contact in it that hadn't buzzed yet, school hadn't started at John Muir yet. I stopped talking but went inside my head in the chatter there, continuing to berate me for going in there. It would tell me at least your twin had sense. You're dirty. Whenever an older man would touch me, I always felt like I was dirty with sand. We got to my sister's house and I found one of her dresses and asked if I could shower and change clothes. She was trying to be the cool big sister and she said yes and asked no further questions. She probably was happy I was getting out of the grown-up mini dress I was wearing.

Trials & Tribulations of Being Gang Raped (Lillian Davis)

Growing up as a young black girl now I can say it was a good and bad thing. For the most part, I was born to a father that was a Blood from East side low bottom Pueblos and a mom that ran in A Trey Gangster hood Crips on Normandie. Life was good between being in the projects. It was like a big family growing up in the project. You played together, fought together and even got your ass whooped together. Everyone knew each other. I learn how to fight going to school and growing up in the projects. That's just how it was. You might have a group of girls that want to try you so either you fight or be laughed at.

Soon one day out of nowhere things started getting to a point where we began to stay with my aunt in the projects because of my parents on drugs. I could not believe this was happening to me. I actually ran away the night we had to move. But I was found and had to move to this new house and La Puente. What I called little Mexico City. There were no female places where I felt like I did not belong. I was being rebellious because I could not understand where my mom and dad were and why I could not be with them. Now in the project there were not as many Mexicans.

It was Cambodian and Black predominantly. So, the Mexicans that were there were friendly. These Hispanics in La Puente were a gang banging cholo in Cholos that hated black's whites in any other race of opposite of them. So, with me being the only black girl in all my classes coming up, my skills of fighting paid off defending myself against them. Besides being mistreated inside the place called home I was being sexually advanced by my blood cousins. They felt it was good to touch on me improperly as I grew and developed. I had a DCFS worker that came due to me and my little sister now being adopted by my aunty.

But they would not be as hard as they are now. My case worker knew what was going on and all she did was tell her to keep her son separate from me. I guess it could have been worse had they removed us and separated my little sister in I out of the home. My mom would always find her way up there for the most part to visit on birthdays and holidays. But then we are not seeing her like that. My sister is about four years younger than me so she was attached to my aunt. As shit started to go bad for us. She was more of their complexion or high yellow banana complexion. So, she blended in with them.

I became the black sheep. I resemble my mom and my dad dark with thick hair and sometimes what you would call defiant. I hate being out there. I concentrated on school and making good grades despite having to fight a lot. I was running track and was an honor roll student. But it would not take away the hurt and pain of wanting my mother back. In between school I will run away from home. I would make up stories because when I said what was going on people looked at me like I was crazy. And when I would run away from home with nowhere to turn to the streets, I would be left outside to sleep on a wooden bench that sat in our yard. Sometimes they would toss me a blanket to cover up if it was cold. Other times I would be looked at through the windows and patio door as I laid outside.

Even my own little sister would watch and laugh at me being outside in the cold. Instead of getting help for me being a child taken from her parents and adopted out and confused. They watched me run away. It just felt like I was in a big old dream. I remember when they gave me a jar of Motrin 800mg pills and watched and helped me take the pills saying it would help me. I ended up being rushed to the emergency room with being public bed I tried I tried to say I did not try and kill myself but I was not believed when I told the truth to how I got the pills in my possession anyway. So, I was transferred to Mental Facility for suicide. After spending time there, I was switched to Charter Oak Metal Facility. Where again, I was one of the only black girls transferred there at the time. So, the Hispanics in there and the white girl started fights with me and with it being more of them and one of me.

I had picked up an anger issue along the way. And some of the staff are not doing their job. That would lead to my first experience of being given the hot shot and being put in the strait jacket at a young age. I remember my family coming to visit me at the facility and due to an altercation earlier I was strapped down to a bed as a result. My family was told that I was an angry child that was constantly fighting with other girls so they had to subdue me. Which was not true. Again, the staff were predominantly Hispanic and a few white staff. So, they were taking sides in playing favoritism with those of their own ethnicity.

I remember coming home and continuing running away and getting caught by my family right before school would end. I remember attending Valley High Continuation School. I was a little around 15 years old. I have been kicked out of school for fighting. I just could not catch a break. So, one day, I was just having a bad morning and was ready to go home and I had just gotten dropped off to school by the school bus. I knew this white girl who was cool. We became friends at the Continuation School. That day she also did not want to stay at school.

So, she had just met a guy she knew that we could go get some weed or something from. I really did not smoke at the time but agreed just to leave the school to go with her period going against the gut feeling telling me it was a bad idea to go with her. But, I did... (I can't remember today's specific details due to my therapist over the years. Saying, I buried the gang rape and other shit so deep that it's like I blinked my memory to a certain extent which is why I have nightmares). I just know the feeling. I felt once inside and now saw that there were multiple Hispanic guys with tattoos tattooed all over their bodies, some showing Puente 13 or however it was spelled in Spanish.

I really don't remember how it all went wrong. It is still all a blur; I remember the first guy on me and wondering how I got here. I remember being rough handled then another Hispanic on top of me. I realized I had put myself in a bad position. I remember blinking in and out. I don't remember if it was from fighting back being hit that cause me to blackout all the repeated sexual offense my body was enduring. But it would be a different guy each time, I would come through and open my eyes. I realized fighting was useless. And I think I just numbed my mind and body as the assault continued. I just remember different Mexicans with different tattoos do what they choose and I could do nothing about it. Meanwhile the girl I was with was being brutally assaulted as well. I could hear her screaming as well. The assault seemed like it was forever.

I don't know exactly nor can I remember how we ended up in the restroom at the same time but we did. Ripped clothing and scared, I knew we only had one chance to escape and that was through a small window which we were on the second floor. Mind you know one came for us screaming no nothing. Mind you we could hear them plotting to kill us once it was done. (So, imagine hearing voices than your life has to be taken because you could identify your assailants). The girl, I was with she was still in shock so it was like, I had to remind her if we did not save ourselves no one would save us and we will be subject to the repeated sexual attach. What seemed like forever was really a matter of seconds.

We decided to jump out the window, landing on the dumpster underneath the bathroom window. And half naked with torn clothes we ran for our lives. Get into the end of the driveway before we notice we are now in a pursuit of our captors.

They were really trying to catch up. Before we knew it, we had to hide in the deep bush with silence and a prayer. We could hear where they went along with other disrespectful names. So, imagine being 15 assaulted repeatedly then listening to your assailant's nearly feet away from you as you hid. But once it was what we thought was clear we took a chance and made a run for it. Again, here we go a white girl in a black girl running half naked for our lives.

A bus happened to be coming down the street just as we were running in damn near and ran in front of the bus in desperation to get away. The bus driver quickly shut the door and asked where we were going as we ducked down on the bus. I remember the bus driver asked if we needed the police and we said no. We were scared, shocked and did not know what they did. She went home off the bus and with the way, I have been treated in mouth forced to home with my auntie, I had no desire to go home I remember getting off the bus clothes still rip the filth of all my assailants it's still up on my body.

Hair scrounges gone. Hair band gone in front of a restaurant called Michael's that sat across from a street called Loukelton which was my Street. I had become friends with a young white lady that was a waitress there. She pulled me into the women's restroom where I broke down crying telling her all that I had just endured. After feeling like it was my fault in the doors of what they would say. I agreed to let her call the police. The police came out and took a statement while they contacted my friend at her house, I again still in my ripped clothing led the police back to where the assault took place.

Funny that the same apartment no longer had anyone in it and when they came out only another young Hispanic lady came to find out it was. Naturally she was taken into custody, belongings that we did not realize we left behind or still in the apartment. My hair scrounges and things that fell out of our pockets were there. But not one of our assailants was there. Except for the evidence in the obvious sign from the house a struggle had gone on. After that, I was taking back to the hospital where pictures in what is called a rape kit test was administrated.

Semen was recovered from inside of me as well as on my clothing. Mind you when they finally did get my friend to the hospital, she had showered all the evidence of her body in lies to her parents. I just felt re violated sitting there having to go through the process of rape victim is endured from the police which were males (Hispanic shall I also say) along with the doctors and staff.

When the police dropped me off to my auntie (who was my adopted mom). I was not hugged, comforted or any of that. I was just left to feel as though I deserved it or that it was my fault and it was never spoken or brought up again. As the result of my rape, I later learned I was pregnant. By this time, I believe I'm 16 years old. After learning of my pregnancy. I was taken by my cousins, adopted brother and sister to an abortion clinic. I remove back in these days they will surround you with pictures back then of what was being done to babies were having abortions and I remember getting scared and falling down on knees praying and a voice said to me listen to me with no questions axe and it will all be OK.

Do not get rid of this baby. In, I got up crying and left the abortion clinic. September 1996, I delivered my beautiful half breed daughter who is now 24 years of age. So embarrassed and young not knowing which of my rapists fathered my daughter, I just gave her a Hispanic last name. I will never know which one fathered my daughter unless they are ever arrested from that gang and their DNA matches the DNA from my rape. Then it will tell which were my rapists and which of them fathered my daughter. I have had a hard time dealing with being brutally gang raped by a Mexican game. I remember not wanting to live.

I remember becoming unable to eat and sleep. I remember running away even more. I could not force it in school. I tried different drugs. I went through the stages of hating Mexicans. I would even rob the perverted ones that will be old in trying to pick me up. I have become out of control. My anger had doubled. I was fighting Mexicans every time I got the chance. It had turned me into someone dangerous at a young age. I felt like every grown man that prayed on me knowing I was a teenager deserved to be robbed for everything they had. At that time, I did not give a fuck. It was almost like some eye for eye type of shit. I was damn near like a deadly assassin.

With all the hurt and pain for my gang rape it has followed me into my present day living. I have been in therapy for years now. I learned; I was molested by a female at the age of five by mentally disturbed girl that had also molested my older cousins as well. My therapist said that, I had suppressed it along with my rape and that is why it came to me in a dream. I suffer from PTSD as well as severe anxiety. I do not like dark places. I get nervous around large groups of men. I hate buses. Because of all that, I went through and felt like I had nothing to offer that would allow me to stay with a person who was mentally and physically abusive for five years.

Being raped is a trauma that haunt you for life. Being gang raped brutally by multiple men an escaping for your life is something you will never escape mentally. It has followed me into my marriage. At Night, I can't sleep with my clothes off. I have been touched in my sleep by my husband just to be tile, I reacted as though he was trying to take it from me. I will wake up with no recollection of anything he's saying. I am hard to trust people after being raped. I had a hard time coping with life, having kids and dealing with PTSD. I have been on meds for depression, anxiety, PTSD, nightmares and other elements left from my attack.

I do not let my daughters go to people's houses. I am super protective knowing what I endured. My goal and mission in life is to teach my daughters and other young black girls and women of my age and older that silence is never best. We do not deserve to be violated anyway and thrown away like garbage dismissed or silence. I was sexually abused by family members and strangers. But no matter how down in the gutter. I fell or I fought to find a reason to get back up. Now at the age of 40. I realized that, I survived and I am a voice for other victims. Some of us never tell our assault in fear and shame.

But I can assure you if you keep the faith and stay true to yourself as the person you are, you will stand firm through it all. The whole black concept of what goes on in my house stays in my house is a cycle which needs to be broken. Silence is more deadly and hurtful and damages you forever. So, if I don't do anything else in life, I want to help young ladies relive their abuse daily but learn how to conquer and get over the aftermath that the trauma causes. We are black queens, young and seasoned queens. We Matter. Our Stories Matter. We are somebody. We are little black girls that rocked into the black queens we are. We will always be traumatized. But no longer are victims. But we no longer are victims. We Are Survivors!

Through It All, I Became a Healer for Young Ladies in Women (Bubbles)

My birth name is Carolyn Lenora Hamilton my nickname is "Bubbles" it is not a street name it was a name my father gave me when I was first born. I carried the name with me to the streets. I am now known by many names (it depends on what hat I am wearing). Minister B, Auntie & Minister Carolyn just to name a few. My story is very real and I'm very fortunate to be alive to tell it. I was shot, stabbed, and hit by a car two years ago on New Year's Day.

I was hit in the head with a hammer for 4xs and God spared my life once again! So, my story is very real. I am now a hard-court street gang Interventional, Prevention, Counselor, Domestic Violence, Author and a Minister. I call myself a street minister because I'm out in the trenches in the hoods on "the hoe track" where woman is prostituting themselves. I cross the state lines going into some of the most dangerous prisons there is to minister the gospel.

I go where it's rough and dirty where nobody else wants to go. I go to help save and win lost souls and redirect them. I am a "West Adams Baby Born and Raised". The set I rep Neighborhood Rollin 20 Bloods. I am not a former gang member because there is no such thing. It's "Blood in Blood out", so basically, I am a retired non active member of the set. My job today is to defuse situations, help assist the youngsters in the hood get their life on track. Do legal work for those behind the wall and stand in the step up when clergy is needed.

I grew up in the hood so I was always a piece of the puzzle myself and my siblings. I was the youngest of 9. I believe I started interacting with the hood life in 1978 but again I was in the hood in 1964 (the day I was born). When I came up with things that were definitely different, we respect our geez meaning we didn't talk back. We listened, we were schooled and we respect all the elders in the hood. There wasn't as much chaos in backbiting in betrayal or wicked stuff going on among the homies. There was loyalty we all ate together, made money together and at times we would literally sleep together without any sexual activity no one was the floor period!

We walked the blocks 10 toes down, we marked our territory and if you were our rivals, you got dealt (with hands not guns). As the years came a lot of things changed, they came with the foolery. It went from a Blood and Crip war to Bloods on Bloods and Crip on Crip. Now homie on homie wars within killings of individual hoods are normal. It's gotten out of hand and it's crazy! I started slowing down when my little bro

"Michael Johnson" (ck Mann) was murdered. I still pushed a line but my heart started changing.

I began to abuse drugs and alcohol in two homies by the name of "Skip Townsend" and "Kenneth Smith" started pulling me into the 2nd call meetings. My mindset then began to change. I was later included in a documentary called "Gang Girls". It showed the screwed-up life of Bubbles and it pissed me off when I saw it on the big screen but it made me want to get myself to get myself together. I packed all my belongings, put them in storage and went to drug rehab in "Action California". That was the beginning of my end.

I came home, I got certified in a couple of things, and started my own organization. I've been doing this for 11 years now. I'm still putting in work for the hood, however I'm no longer gang banging. I'm a community activist and I give to the hood and not take from it. My advice to any young lady is to get your education and don't get caught up. My parents paid 12 years of hard-earned money to put me through private school and I went a totally different direction than what they expected from me. These young ladies have to think with their minds and don't be with just "Any Man but a Gentleman".

I was married five times to 5 different gangsters and in all 5 ended up with life sentences! They had different names but the same damn game. Don't sell your soul to the street or to the first man that says he loves you "God" loves you and he is the man with the master plan. I would tell any young lady to follow his lead and let God order his steps.

Through Trial & Error I Stood by His Side (Juelz)

I have known Julius for quite some time since we were teenagers running around trying to find our purpose in this world. We grew up differently but also the same just follow different paths. One would wonder why two completely opposite people find common ground and grow to become brothers not just friends. Well, I can't even answer that question myself but I don't need an answer either. I'm just happy to be in love with my brother, that's all that truly matters.

In 2005 he went away to jail (wrong place, wrong time scenario). Over a year or so later, I went to his sentencing and heard the judge's verdict and that shook a tree. I just tried to always remind him of that day, so when he finally comes home to remember that he'll never go back. Yes, he made the wrong choices in life. We all do but I did not see that as a reason to just leave him all alone suffering in prison with no connection to the outside world. Keeping that hope and imagination alive, living vicariously through my letters, imagining what I'm seeing every day.

Throughout his time incarcerated, I lived in Atlanta, Georgia and was a college student trying to find out what I really wanted to do with my life through the education I was receiving. I bounced around through different schools but finally went back to what I loved as a kid and that is art work (Graphic Design) which I graduated with four awards. I worked in the club for some years while at school and after, graduated until it shut down. Worked a few jobs awkwardly and now I'm working for a school system out here but not during the pandemic.

I created a business of my own to finally have something I can call my own with no one calling the shots besides myself. I control everything alone. It's not a big business but I have aspirations that will become one day. It still has full control and ownership of it. It's called "Star Moss Wellness" and it forces on building and improving the overall health of the human body with natural herbs from the earth from other countries where it is pure and natural. It was a real journey trying to figure out what I want to do in life and it still is because things in life always change in very expected changes like the one. The entire world is enduring now.

For those of you, youth that's like us trying to figure it out, I don't know if you'll ever make it to college don't even worry about that. I highly recommend trade school because you'll get in and out the door and two years with a trade and skills. And jobs lined up and you can take from that and build your own brand. Established business ownership there's nothing like owning your own. The brother standing before you known as Julius Jones is a good brother. He just made some mistakes in his life and is turning it around for the betterment of himself. His kids are in the community to steer you all in the right direction. I watch him go from a young boy to a grown man making the right steps in the right direction. The past was just stepping stones; we were all a product of our environment; it just affected us in different ways to one day reach new heights.

Becoming A Deacon Was Destiny (Charles)

I was tired of everything I was into. I was addicted to alcohol, PCP, black and mild's, women, cursing, stealing etc.... I was even tired of being addicted to the hood. I was having fights with a lot of homies, some of them day ones that we should have never fought in life! I was tired of me; I was the problem. But I knew that no AA meeting or self-help group could help me. I knew I needed prayer. I went to the church and prayed. The Pastor that prayed to me said that after that prayer, I would never be the same.

I haven't been the same since 2007. I wrote my book because it was so supernatural! God really showed up, abs changed me for real and saved my soul. I knew that God was real, but didn't know that much power was available to us! And that we could talk to him back and forth like a real person and he answers! Didn't know we could have a real relationship with the living Almighty God! I also wrote the book because so many people are lost in that gang lifestyle.

I pray that my story will bless someone. Help someone make a decision to serve Jesus Christ! There's a better way and people need to know it! It's not only a better way to live, but we have assurance to live with Jesus for eternity after this life! It's the best decision, hands down, that I've ever made in my life! Me becoming a Deacon is another story. I was from Fruit Town Brims. When I was gang banging, I used to deal with this girl from the Swans Blood Gang off the East Side.

When I would go to a house and her mother was there, she would pray for me. Her mother was really into God! She would always call me "Deacon Charles", she said, I was going to be a" Deacon". Me and her daughter didn't pay her any mind. Knowing the things that I was into. I have French braids in my hair with khakis on. I was Banged Out!

I was far from being a part of anybody's church and it did know the first thing about being the Deacon. The girl's mother had passed away some time before I had gotten saved. About two years later, I got saved. I was ordained as a deacon in the church. So, I changed my name on Facebook and put Deacon in front of it. The girl that I used to deal with from Swans sent me a message and said," If my mother could only see you now. That's when it dawned on me that she used to call me Deacon all the time! I give God the glory because she really knew the lord! She wasn't just talking.

Giving Back Henry Snyder (Julius Jones)

I was beyond honored to receive the certificate from a High School. I once attended Henry Snyder. I didn't walk the stage, my guidance counselor Mr. Murray felt best, I attended night school because he wanted to see me finish school. Mr. Murray said, stay in two much more dramatic instruments in gang life. So, on the first day of school of my senior year, he mentions Adult School. Honored because countless teachers saw me as a failure, troubled student. Never offer a helping hand, just always judge me. Couldn't blame them for looking at me differently, I stay suspended my average attendance in school 59 days a year. To mentor Freshman through Senior year was a blessing. I can actually say, I gave back not only to not follow in my footsteps. Yet informed, these future graduates have a plan at the age they are at now. You don't plan to fail; you fail to plan.

College is not for everyone: find a trade, find out what you love the most. That's your passion and turning it into a goal, may take time yet the steps you make if that's what you love then you will succeed! Get your license from that trade, sell yourself to your family. Do free jobs to market yourself, build a table for example for your aunt. You know if you do a great job your aunt will inform everyone, she knows your work.

You can become a Carpentry, Nail Tech, Registered Nurse, Cosmetology, Plumbing, Electrician, Criminal Justice, painting etc.... Have to start having these new generations back using their minds and hands. Instead of shaking their asses in videos, men are trying to prove to everyone else how real they all are, how about being yourself!

Everything Is Not Always What It Seems (Big Sha)

Watching the older dudes from around the way in my neighborhood, had a single mother she couldn't really afford anything extra. I went to what I saw around me, which was the streets. I was put on the Fruit Town Militant Minded Brim. The unity at one time, it was like a roller coaster, it was good and it was bad but I tried to be consistent with it at all times going through that process.

Gang wars is like, I don't know you can't really explain it man, it is brain reckoning, heartbreaking if I heard from some homies not all of them. I don't wish prison on anybody, it is just like the streets, you got to do what you have to do to maintain that respect and I did for 12 years. Currently wrapping it up now in the halfway house. Nowadays being a Damu is a fake. Just a fashion show at this point, something to be a part of so everybody is just doing it. I would just want to let them kids and teenagers know shit isn't always what it seems on the outside looking in. You know you got people amongst you who did a lot of time already. So, you don't have to walk down that vicious path we have already been through, so we can make a better way for the youth.

My Family Counting on Me (Top Shelf)

Growing up in Jersey City as a kid made me grow up fast, I saw a lot early so it got me ready for life a lot sooner. Well, my household was a little hectic, I experienced drugs, violence, and still had love all under the same roof. I loved school early on and didn't want to miss a day and yes, I had hoop dreams before the void of having to provide took over.

Well, my mom went to jail when I was nine years old so from then on, I had to live with relatives and that's when things took a turn for the worst. I had no father to go to for guidance so the streets became my mother and father. I didn't know at first that, I was participating in the genocide culture to me my gang was my extended family. When, I came aware that it was genocide, I started doing my part to make better choices for myself and my homies.

Well getting put on to my set Fruit Town Militant Minded Brim. Meant that, I took a stand on loyalty to those who were a part of the same struggles as, I as well another branch of family. In having Emanuel in Julius a part of the set which are two of the most "Solid Brothers" I've met in my 36 years of living. I was in the 4th grade and they never changed who they were as people. That's so big in the times we live in, people get very different, they are more like my brothers and will always remain in my life.

Honestly speaking, I was already in the streets with many followers, my set opened up doors around the world so, I felt connected to a bigger entity. I have a young lady; I often think how I would react to her dealing with a gang banger. I would think that she's looking for a guy like her father. My reaction would simply be that my daughter helped him grow into the best version of himself. Of course, I've been through wars; anybody who picked a side has been in a war.

If we go through emotions as well in prison, they are politics and things to keep in store... The difference from state and federal prison is you deal with people all over the world, so you see all cultures, all ways of banging and get to see a different overall perspective and federal prison. My outlook changed; I wanted more out of life than these concrete walls. I'm the backbone for my family and being away from them causes them to search for strength and guidance in the wrong places.

My motivation for business came from my ambition to win! Even when I did wrong in my life it was to live better. So, I decided I wanted to do something that no one could take from me and my family would be set from the street wasn't an option. My plans are to open my own clothing line in a brand and also open a detail shop in my neighborhood. Wanted to rearrange my life, I got to show those who followed me a different route and so they know it's OK to come from what we come from and be successful. We'll put their kids into sports that can be effective or things to keep them active. If any parents don't want their child going down the same path as me, I have started with communication even more, overall, with your child and knowing what he or she is into you may be able to get a hold on them. The choice is still ultimately going to be who has the bigger influence on the child.

Bloods and Crips Peace Treaty Out Harlem New York

Oyg Redrum 781 from Inglewood Avenue, Piru Gang. Flew in from Watts, California to Harlem, New York to document and film for his assistant wanting the Blood and Crips peace treaty. Julius from Fruit Town Brims 30s thirty-six street was informed by Oyg Redrum 781 about the two sides meeting at a park. Yet the day with the weather turned out bad.

So, Julius informs Oyg Redrum781 he may have a place where the Bloods and Crips can meet up. Jason Davis from Original Blood Brothers lived in Harlem, New York. Jason is a Credible Messenger where he helps redirect young teenagers' lives in countless speaking events and traveling to different high schools to educate. Whether they are in gangs or not at the "Living Redemption Youth Opportunity Hub" and also help out with the communities.

The call was made by Julius to Jason about what was supposed to take place. Jason was excited for himself in Julius either one of them didn't even know he was going to be taking place. Jason made a few phone calls. And now it was said to be at" Living Redemption Youth Opportunity Hub" Harlem, New York on May 7th 2019.

Julius introduced himself. I was put onto Fruit Town Brims thirty 36th St. I'm from Jersey City, New Jersey. If I told everyone I agree with them, then I don't. Everyone was just quiet then others looked as if that was the reason I am even there. It should be started off as a cease fire. By starting off as a ceasefire then necessary steps can be worked on step by step. Having a peace treaty is starting at A and going straight to Z. Every Damu set has homies setting each other up and killing each other. Same for the Keeyway sets.

How can there be peace when there is no peace amongst them? You have to clean your own backyard first. Having a ceasefire creates agreements that the guns are down. You stay on your side and they stay on their side. With respect, when seeing one another. Give each set to work on their own peace within. Also start holding older men accountable, passing on the wrong information to the younger generations.

Guide them to start respecting the elders more, even more so Respecting themselves. Start holding block parties for the kids, giving water park rides, Rent-A-Center has events for the kids. Start helping elders with the groceries, if they don't need help then hold the door. Put effort in hustlers not selling drugs in front of the kids, even residents that paid their taxes there or else it's just trespassing. I also expressed a Jew would walk pass and all everyone would do would just laugh at how they all dress.

So, you have to ask, why are you laughing? Where you're standing on the block right, every day 24/7 for how many years? What time is it? Isn't it after 10:00 PM you are on the block all day, still haven't made enough right? They walk past every day without any worries and do you know why? Everyone caught up on materialism, the Jews owned blocks at a time, apartment buildings, multiple houses within 2/3 years.

Countless people have been on the corner most of their life yet still have nothing but what? You and you would get at a person that looks like you, broke as you and start mugging at the person that is you! Walking around paranoid from a place you grew up in your old life? Again, the Jews being here for how long again, walking around without a care in the world. Nobody sees the problem? We are not just gangs, we as a culture are the problem.

We really need to unlearn and relearn, if we're going to make it to another generation. All in competition with one another in still have nothing, countless too busy trying to outdo the next. Not realizing they missed a whole lot of steps themselves. I was also informed about a particular Blood set. It was long overdue that New York NYBBA Brims and New Jersey West Side Brims connected. Not planning it becomes more authentic.

I decided the peace treaty was the right time. Be truthful and honest, both states had some similarities of being misled, guided, and lied to for personal agendas in greed. No matter who, when and how things started. The reality of this "Lifestyle" is a "Deathstyle". Countless lives have been wasted, lost to prisons, paralyzed even in death.

I Westside Fruit Town Brims 36 St meeting Peewee from NYBBA 59 brims there wasn't no anger, agendas, trying to downplay one another we had a common goal is to guide and teach these younger generation that if you a "Damu" move from the heart and start carrying yourself like 1. Uplift your brother in sister from another instead of bashing each other. Start feeding the less unfortunate instead of dumping your communities with poison, then turn around saying you love your hood.

Protect it by helping the elderly, stop blasting music when the citizens that live in the apartment buildings are trying to rest for tomorrow and have to get up in the AM for work. Need more book bags, turkey drives, throw free skating bus trips, bowling contests the kids' actively busy so they will have a better future. This is history: decades of hatred between two states in reality both fell victim to a bunch of lies....

Holding Accountability (Massacre)

Growing up I was into sports. I wasn't the greatest basketball player, Yet, I was very good at football. Football is where I flourished until the temptation of the streets took hold. Also being from a neighborhood, I had the privilege of being raised around musicians" Naughty by Nature" so of course like any other youngsters in my community. I tried to pick up the microphone. The hours in the studio didn't compare to the thrill of hanging out in hustling, so the rest was history to the corners I went to. As a kid, I dream of being the next Emmitt Smith, the next Deon Sanders. Growing up it was unlikely that we saw influential black role models who weren't on the TV screen for sports or music. Dreams consisted of being like those in my neighborhood who had community celebrity hood riches. You know the girls, the clothes and the cash. My dreams later in life manifested into a 30-year federal nightmare. The streets were sort of what it always was of me.

I was taken straight from the hospital to the project. From projects to Carnegie Ave where, I could step right outside my door and watch the dope boys getting money. Where I could see with my own eyes the perks of the streets. Once I hit middle school my grades started to slip. My parents made it clear that a bad grade's equivalent to basic living. The Jordan's the whole fashions were a no go. What they didn't know was up until that point. I have become accustomed or rather known for being the next youngster on the rise.

So, I had to go out and get it to be able to keep up with the street's expectations. Growing up in my environment, we were always something. We were always out slanging and banging but it wasn't until I was 13 years old, that the grit actually took shape. Prior to that age it was more my block this, my click that. We even have little gangs inside the neighborhood but in 1993 it became all about Queen St Inglewood, CA to Ill town, New Jersey. Before being put onto the set we didn't actually have structured that wasn't how we were run.

However, those in charge were those who put in the most work. Those who were the most reputable. Every hood comes with those who do a little more, make more funds than the others, care about the turf more passionately. Those were the ones at the" top" per say. We respected older homies in the neighborhood and amongst each other. We respect one another after respect is earned. For my particular neighborhood back in the day we were run differently because we were all from the same environment, same community.

Our neighborhood mirrors that of our West to the point of, you couldn't be from set if you weren't from turf. You couldn't run Queen Street... If you weren't bleeding on the Q. Other sets, though I love them all, were run a bit differently to the point of, you could be from anywhere per se, and run this set. So, you could stroll then run into home from the same set "slanging and banging" in two or three different areas. With us, it was the 10th Streets and that was it.

Oh, today there's a huge difference in the way things are today and how they were in the early 90's. In the early 90's on the East Koast, Blood up and coming something rare, new, disliked that even somewhat most hated.

To be a Blood back then, you had to really be willing to put it all on the line. You had to truly love the gang. Gang culture wasn't understood on the East Koast in the 90's. To many it was something strictly from California, and to be doing something of the sort, you were looked at as an imitator, a faker. With the majority of the streets holding this view when you stepped out the door you had to be willing to perform. You had to be ready to make this thing which was hated into something or respected.

That struggle in itself brought about unity with all sets. It was that feeling of "us against the world". Today says are at war with each other. The unity seems to have faded things that ignited beef, thus and so what seems to foster that divide is" individualist's ideologies." The banner is almost done away with. Out East that just isn't how we were raised. I walked and talked, slanging and banged with big homies from every set. Today not only our younger homies disrespect reputable people from other groups. They are reckless to the point of disrespecting big homies from their very own set.

The unity seems to be misplaced. Wars come with the territory. I believe if you are involved in the streets, then war is inevitable. You don't necessarily have to go looking for trouble, trouble will most certainly find you. When the bullets start flying in the back and forth it appears to be a day and night thing. Then you are at war. I remember coming into the system, younger people still hyped up on the thrill of gang wars, an older homie told me. When you are at a certain age, if you aren't calling for peace, then you have never known war. In the culture the loss of homies, even home girls, become commonplace.

So much so that the trauma is beginning to lose its effect. You began believing that death is natural. Being in the back pews of a church while a mother buries her child. You become immune to it. No mistaking, the love ceases to exist, the painful tune of death resonates, yet the crushing feeling of defeat lessons with each funeral you attend. Personally, I have never been shot, but I have been stabbed. I have lost plenty of loved ones. I remember being only 16 when one of my closest homies from the set was killed by another homeboy from the set.

I called the streets a little while ago, and got the news that a young girl of mine from another set was killed as a result of gun violence. I'm not here to speak negatively about the culture. For I'm deeply in love with the "one way" and the" righteous way". The way which speaks to us is uplifting, protecting, providing for and supporting our communities. Thus, amidst the few positives, there is a long line, and history of negative outcomes associated with the culture and as a parent or an older figure to my younger relatives.

I believe I have a duty and obligation to steer them away from any harm possible. As a result of the hurt, I know it is associated with life. I would not want my children or younger relatives to enter this life. Surely this sounds contradictory to some, however, since my days as a child. I remember my parents telling me how they always wanted better for me and my brother. So, in turn that is my mindset. Allow me to endure the pain and suffering so those after me won't.

Well damn, I was never allowed to walk an actual prison yard. I spent the entire four years of my state sentence in solitary confinement. Due to being a highly influential member of the Bloods. When I got to the federal penitentiary, I walked in with a chip on my shoulder. I had something to prove outside of my respective neighborhood, city and state. And so, my early years were filled with a bit of trouble. Trips to the whole, more time spent in solitary confinement, a special management unit. What was eye opening to me was how I ran with hundreds of Bloods, yet the culture differed. The "one way" remains. However, the Bloods in New York did it differently from the Bloods in New Jersey.

The Bloods in the South did it differently than the Bloods in the Midwest, and the homies out West did it differently than the homies out East. School for us wasn't a priority. Actually, the school we attended was an enemy hood, so an innocent trip to school would often end up in fights for our lives. During school hours we were out hustling, smoking, drinking, young teenagers with little to no direction but when the older homies came through, we had to roll or face the consequences. The home girls in my view are all my sisters. The love I have for them is 1, I would have for one coming out of my mother's womb.

Gang culture is male dominated so for a female to be thorough enough to ride it out with the homies. And put on for the set, she was thorough enough to be respected. The home girls from my set were feminine, common somewhere out there like the homies. And if a homie disrespected, she demanded the fade. I've witnessed a home girl or to tighten up a homie for disrespecting. There were some romantic relationships between homies, and home girls and at the time they got a little messy but overall, the love for the turf remained mutual.

Respect the hood and the hood respects you! This goes for both homies and home girls. Well recently I just wrote my second book. In August I did my first annual school supply giveaway to the youth in my community. This year it was small, but I had plans to pick up my momentum as time went on. I just want to show a different look, change the stereotypes, the negative stigmas about myself and other gang members. As in everything, there are some good and some bad. Now that I'm in my 40's for me it's all about giving back. Educating the next generation, bringing awareness to not only the gang culture but the culture of African Americans as a whole.

My two children are grown, neither is involved in life and I thank Allah daily for that. Since being imprisoned. I have secured my G.E.D alcohol and substance abuse courses to enroll in college. Correspondence among a list of other things. I haven't let the time do me. I've chosen to do the time. I would say I'm most definitely at a point where it's put up or shut up. Leading by example, a positive example this goes around.

People join sets for different reasons. Some for the familial bond. Sum to secure what they may be lacking in the home. I don't necessarily feel it's the set that makes a person bad. Yet what a person does that creates the negative. Still to answer your question, I wouldn't recommend a child joining a set or a teenager. As we know biologically, a child doesn't have the mental capacity to fully interpret right from wrong, thus and so their decisions can be negatively influenced.

The ability to rationalize, compartmentalize, and analyze isn't at full scope, and for those reasons. I would not and could not recommend a child or teenager to make such a crucial decision. For those parents trying to keep their children in the right direction. Understand the importance of time. As parents some have a gift in the form of a love language. They brought their children to Jordan's, the new Louis Vuitton. The new Fendi, but lacking in the gifting of time. You have to build with your child. See what's on their mind, inventory, their friends, check in with their teachers, and most definitely find that balance between being a friend and a parent.

When my children were growing up, coming out would emphasize my circumstances being imprisoned for 30 years. Then I would express to them that the consequences of their actions were theirs to bear. I can't live out your mistakes. If the cops come calling, I can't go to prison for you. If someone gets too shooting because you're out in the streets. I can't take that bullet for you. Make them see the downside of rushing into adulthood before their proper time. Most importantly, we have to educate our children. Push them towards their purpose. Champion day greatness. Lastly shower them with love. You will be surprised how many of our youth turn to the streets because they feel in their home there is a lack of love.

Product Of My Environment
(Big L)

I was born in Jersey City, NJ on November 4th 1983 two Denise Harvey who's my mother and Sam Leak my father both of them are dead now. I grew up in a lot of different cities and states as a child or mother was born in New York, well my father was born in North Carolina. So, I moved around a lot coming up, I saw things that most children should never see. I watched my mom's getting raped at the age of five.

Being a baby boy of four my second oldest brother was in a car accident the same year a few months later my father killed himself playing with a gun. And the twisted thing is when my mother told me he was dead. I don't even shed a tear! And he was very well active in my life, I mean I guess I was too young to understand the world at that time. But growing up in the streets of New York and Jersey City it hardens the heart to death as do you see it so much around you.

But as I got older, I watched my uncles doing their thing in the streets of Jersey City. I always wanted to be like them because they had the respect, the money, the girls but they wouldn't allow me to hang or be around them and made me go to school. The first School, I went to was on Union Street in Jersey City, New Jersey PS# 14. I mean the drug dealers were right outside the school on every corner we turned to violence etc.! That always made me even more curious to what it would be like to be in the street. I mean it was crazy but I didn't last and that school being a little knucklehead.

I was removed from there and sent to PS# 15 on Stegman Street on the hill in Jersey City, NJ where things took its turn and my life on the street gave me the name Big L. Yeah, at the age 10, I received the name in the streets known for having guns, known to shoot first ask questions later man, I can't even begin on how it all started. But it happened going to PS# 15 school, I dropped out in the 4th grade. I mean for real; I told myself fuck school. I'm Big L! I don't need school, not knowing it will hurt me in my future. Growing up in and out of Youth Detention Centers. Jamesburg etc....

I really didn't know how to read or write. I literally had to teach myself all those things over the years being incarcerated. My life is like a lifetime movie, I really don't know how to explain it most people would have had to be there to know or understand it. I decided to join the Nine Trey Gangster Blood out of the Bronx, New York when I was around 11 years old. Following behind my big cousin who was a part of the gang himself.

After years of being with the Nine Trey, I've learned that I was misled by their leaders. I was 19 years old when I was in a Northern State Prison gang unit in Newark NJ. When I met a guy by the name BG out of Paterson NJ. I mean real love gangster. We actually met down in Jamesburg when I was 13 years old but in the northern state where we got close, he taught me the things. I once was taught that gang was not real and introduced me to the Fruit Town Brims 36 street area out of Westside South Central L.A. He broke down the differences between the two Coasts and explained to me he himself was once a part of the East Coast set. Sex Money Murder I never understood the difference between sets. I always thought we moved as one. As time went on in my life, I came to realize everyone that said their Blood is not a Blood just because one wears a red flag throwing up a B. Doesn't it mean their Blood.

It's sad to say but it's true if I knew all the things I know now. I would've been much smaller about getting put on the set. A lot of people in the world will never understand this B Gang. Most of the world looks at us as monsters, scumbags or just a piece of shit. But the reality is that we are humans just like anyone else, some of us never had a choice to do anything else outside of gang banging. Like me for example, I have Big Brothers to look up to but they have never been around. My father died when I was six years old. My mother ran the street's in did whatever she had to do to feed me and my loved ones.

So, the big homies became my Big Brothers, my father's etc. Like the guy BG I was telling you guys about. He became my Big Brother. He taught me so much about this Westside Brim Gang. He taught me that more than homies were brothers' families. Then he introduced me to Og No Good who was from South Central L.A who also brought the light to Fruit Town Brim in New Jersey. I can sit here all day about Og no good LOL....

Mann was like everyone's God at one point he taught us what it was like to bang this set not rep the set. In, I say that with facts it's a difference between gang banging to set and representing your set. He used to tell us shit that had a lot of us like wow to actually hear an Og from California speak on something that we believe in. In that we bang with something that most gang bangers from the East dreamed of at that time. I mean he had our ears in his hands. What he said everyone believed without question.

At that time if that man jumped, we as young gangsters would ask how high. Lost can't even explain what we were, most of us at that time didn't move without that man's word. We felt like without him we were lost. As time went on with me being imprisoned. I've been through so much shit labeled food a few times one of those times. I had fools saying, I told my case. Which was funny to be asked though, I got the most time out of my codefendants. And I plead guilty to all the charges to let them fool go home while I sat in prison for 18 years and seven months in 21 days of my life. They were home with their kids, girls, family etc....

And not one time did, ask for anything or expect anything from them. I dealt with it as a gangster. But most of my homies knew the truth so, I made it out of that situation. Another time, I was considering leaving the Westside Brims for another West Coast set of the Neighborhood Rollin 20's Bloods which was one of the worst things you can do leaving one set for another. Was called set hopping but again my real homies knew and knew the truth. I'm Westside Fruit Town Brims 36st until my eyes close. I mean it's a tattoo all over my body, my life story. I loved them. Westside Brims words can't even explain what I did and will do for the set.

At that time Og No Good was still the man that everyone listened to when he said hands off when he said L Brim good hands off. When I told you I still went hard for the set, I went home. I went to prison at 18 with a 30-year sentence for murder about that time was January 5th 2002. I caught more cases while in prison for stabbing's assault just for disrespecting Westside Brim. We were a Force One movement and one move we all moved. As the time went on federal cases was built behind disloyal, dishonest, weak ass niggas that got put on a set like this nigga name Kasim Mason str8 up cheese eater was wearing a fucking wire.

Another cheese eating by the name Los, can't even tell you that full name. I never even held a conversation with that nigga. But these 2 dudes got some good solid brothers sitting behind them cold walls for the lies they told for a long-time man that shit deep. Just to name a few soldiers that fell behind them cheese eating nigga lies Killa E stand up, BG stand up nigga killer Reek standup nigga and list goes on. Now, I was talking about this dude No Good. Yes, yawl notice I didn't put Og in front of that shit because once the federal charges started being handed down, he folded like a piece of paper.

This whole time he taught us not to be a snitch. Shit our mothers already told us growing up he became the main one snitching on everybody else for the fuck ups he did his got damn self. Yeah, I said it the fool that we once worship became a fucking cheese eating buster. Then to top it all off he never was an Og as he claimed to be. When we all found that out a lot of us were hurt more than others because we really put our lives' freedom for this Westside Brim Gang!

And this shit is facts no made-up shit so, I tell you kids out there that want to get out on this set or that want to follow behind your mentor the big nigga that you look up to is not always who they say they are trust me. I've been up and down in this gang world, and I've seen the good, the bad and the ugliest shit happen. Like, I said my life is like a movie. The only people that will ever understand me are those who live and walk in the gang world. No Good put a lot of our lives online making us believe that he was someone he wasn't. No Good was a straight up piece of shit he really had all of us fooled to the point of a lot of shit I won't say in the book due to the law. But shit was done to put on for the set man. I mean, I have been through so many wars behind this man.

The Brims vs Nine Trey Gangster Bloods war, Brims vs Pirus war, Brims vs G Shine war, Brims vs Sex Money Murder war, Brims going at G Shine & Sex Money Murder at same war, Brims going at Duke Line and Mob Pirus at the same as we'll always going at Crips. Brims vs Neighborhood Rollin 20's Bloods etc.... A lot of good homies in home girls lost their freedom in life due to these wars for real. This is why I'm here to tell these kids out here that they want to Gang Bang. And that wanting to get put on the set is not worth your blood, sweat or tears once you die or in prison for the rest of your life. Your homies forget about you and all you did for the set. Out of 100 homies you may get 2 real ones that do shit for you or your family 2 times. I mean it's crazy how the gang world goes, it used to be structured where as though you had your leaders that earned their spot that know the gang put on for the gang. Now its babies are grown as babies LOL....

I mean you got 20-year-olds saying their Triple OG's Lol.... I thought Triple OGs would be in their 60's 70's etc.... But gang life has changed nowadays; there is no loyalty, honor amongst a set, after going through all the wars. I've been through gang life. I now mentor kids to stay away from this life. I work like a civilized person in my community. A lot of my homies at home are no longer with me. And as I say back in decades those 18 years seven months and 21 days of my life. I've realized if I would be a part of the community the right way. I will end up just like them or spend the rest of my life in someone's hell hole.

And I tell you young men and women are not worth your freedom or life. So always remember this if you don't listen to anything else. I said we declare our own destiny in that destiny comes from the choices we make so think before you act or want to join a gang. Your life will no longer belong to you who will become the set or it will become the state prison system. You will never be the same, trust me. One of my eldest once told me every man and woman desires respect and wealth and fame. What they are willing to pay for is the question they never ask themselves. The most important part, I will leave you with, if everyone says they were until they do something fake then what happens next after they do some fake shit? So, think about that before you get put on the set. I love you all to stay safe, stay smart and stay aware of your choices. Sign out Mr. L Brim Westside Fruit Town Brims 36st until my eyes close....

Young Lost Soul (Rico)

My name is Edwin Fernandez better known to my homies as Miller Rico. I'm originally from Brooklyn NY. I lived there until I was 16 years old. I got introduced to gangs while living there through my brothers and friends. My brothers were all mainly Latin kings or Neta's my homie Benji they also called the homie King Capo and he was G Shine.

The way they were moving made me feel a sense of belonging due to the fact of me jumping from foster care and orphanage homes. And constantly being abused by my foster parents in a jump by Crips on my way from school. I was getting fed up and tired. I felt like no one was there for me and refused to listen and that's the key. I feel just listening to your kids because you might not have all the answers, listening to your child and how he feels might give you a better understanding on how to help them.

But one day while fighting some Crips at the bus stop, I was being beaten an inch away from my life and the homie Capo and a couple of brothers helped me. They chased them off and beat them with sticks. They helped me up. Took me to elderly woman who was respected in the hood named China and she nursed me back to health. accounting faced my foster mother with those bumps and scrapes, all she would have done was beat me. I was tired of feeling alone but at the time I was doing walks with four single mothers and was passing out diapers and things they might give to children handing out food and stuff.

I fell in love with the movement behind that because I was uplifting the person from my hood or society. You might never know that one action of positivity or love might change that person's mentality or give them hope in wanting to do something with their life. It might even stop them from committing suicide but then I ended up getting into trouble with the law due to a big gang fight. I was in the train station with some Crips and my mom sent me to Virginia with my brother who was a contractor for the Navy.

And like always I started hanging around homies but I never got down because I started seeing homies. Badly influencing little homies to do things they probably wouldn't do themselves and it was like the righteous homies we're doing their own thing and that's what, I can say too a little homie. He joins an organization only if he wants to. And why I say that is because I can't control another person from doing what he wants but I can also say this. You don't have to be a part of something to make a change or be looked up to.

If you do join, choose your homies wisely. And keep in mind if a person is not beneficial than they are artificial always keep people in your circle that think like you or better than you. That will elevate you. Trust me, I know I lost my homie Damu at 17 years old and went over there to shoot the individual that killed him. It caused me 10 years of my life from a young age. When I went to prison, I saw everything that changed me from this passive kid.

Who wanted acceptance in just to be loved too lion because there were gang riots. People getting stabbed police beating you up an individual's getting raped and there isn't no running you couldn't escape. Even get alone time for a Peace of Mind. It drives you insane to be away from loved ones and miss out on things in life. Like getting to enjoy prom or buying my first car and playing sports. Everything a kid enjoys in life.

One thing, I can say that I achieved was getting my high school diploma but I got it in prison and wasn't able to see no one there to watch me walk across that stage. So, if you don't want to be that person or lose people to the streets or wake up and get on the prison phone. And here people are dying and can't attend funerals. I suggest you change your situation and the thing that bothers me most is that kids don't want to hear it but wish they did when all these things come crashing down upon them.

As parents, I want to say as far as when it comes to your children listen to them and be calm. Try not to come at them with anger or aggression. As human nature you have to understand we have a fight or flight defense mechanism. So as a child we either went shut down or met you back with the same aggression and that's what led me into the streets. Constantly being screamed at and beaten by my first appearance made me look for acceptance and love somewhere else.

Which led me into being in gangs, which led me getting involved in gang wars in losing homies after homies after homies. I remember when I was living in Virginia Beach and I was walking to the food line and ran into some MS 13s and my little sister was with me. And I had to tell her to keep walking and act like she doesn't know me. I turned around and got into a fight with them and Food Lion. I just walked home holding on to my sister as she cried. And watching over my shoulder to see if they were following me.

Led me into buying a gun which led me into using it and that right there goes to show you being nothing but escalating more and more. Then you find yourself, somewhere you wish you don't want to be. It's up to you to catch it. You don't have to listen to this, if you don't want to. I promise you, when you find yourself somewhere you don't want to be. You would have wished you did go, and succeeded in respecting our women. Without our women there will be no men and just cause a female does not respect herself doesn't mean you should disrespect her more.

You should uplift her; I came home to my brother who is a Gangster Disciple and he has been here more than my own homies have. Watching him suffer due to his little brother being killed by gun violence. R.I.P little Steve and it makes no sense the last little bro kept saying before he passed, he was tired. He was doing the right thing and was really trying hard to get his life on the right track. But I was tired of the obstacles in suffering he was facing and all I can say is in honor of him please don't get tired. There are days that I feel that way and to honor my homie's brother is to not get tired. I hope this message opens your eyes to the reality of the world. This isn't a music video. It damn sure isn't a movie. I have lost so many of my homies that I hate cemeteries. I lost ten years to the system that I will never get back. It is real and it's very serious. It is up to you to decide where you want to be. I leave as I come.... peace.... Rico Miller Es MGB 120 Athens Park Blood's 120th and South Avalon South Central L.A

It's More About Me Than Being from Piru

Trapper John West side, 151 St Original Block Piru. I was born in 1987 in a neighborhood known as Compton Vario Stentas (CV70) in Compton CA. I'm the youngest of my two siblings. Me and my family moved around for some years up until the age of 6 before coming back to Compton. Within those six years I lived in Moreno Valley, Atwater and Los Angeles. Coming back, we moved to a neighborhood known as 135 Piru a couple of years later we moved to Spook Town Compton Crip.

By the time high school came around my parents went their separate way. An I choose to live with my mother on the north side of Long Beach in a neighborhood known as Sex Money Murder Crip. As far as my living conditions within the household, well it was bittersweet. Unfortunately, I grew up in a household where domestic violence and abuse was common. Seeing your parents physically assault one another is very traumatizing.

There was love in the household, just in a way I was too young to understand, I guess. My father was very abusive. Especially towards my older brother. The fight between my father and brother was horrific. Honestly my whole family will fight each other, verbally and physically. I had to witness these events being the baby out of the family not understanding what's going on, nor understanding the feelings and emotions at the time. And not realizing how subconsciously this will become a cycle if I don't change this when I'm older.

The fights between my brother and father stood out the most. Honestly because I looked up to my brother more than my own father. We never wanted for anything financially at all. My mother and father were great providers. But our father didn't take the time to show us how to be men. Not the methods he used when he was around. My father was always in and out. So, I spend more time with my brother who is 7 years older.

He was the only male figure I had around for a long time. And he had the same issues and then some. I was looking up to my brother and my brother is looking up to the gangsters, gang members, thugs, players and pimps we see every day outside our window. Walking to and from school, grocery shopping, going out to eat, any and everywhere that's what we saw and gravitated towards. My brother basically taught me all the wrong shit basically. How to hold a gun, smoke weed, be around drugs, ride around different gang neighborhoods, older women etc....

This is from 7 to 14 years old. My brother is from East Side Blood Stone Villain Gang 56th St. Of course, I'm watching all of the Banging on Wax videos, Piru Love, Damu Rida's, Stead Dipping daily on TV in my room. I sneak ordered videos on the channel called "The Box". So, I was around the gang culture 24/7, sad shit. I touched on the environment briefly, the environment was bitter sweet as well. Of course, the violence I've witnessed all my life. I remember every place we moved to in Compton, I found some type of shell casing or bullets lying around. Bullet holes in the walls, dead bodies in the alleys walking to and from school. My house was shot up, my best friend was shot in front of my house.

Riots at the Compton Parade, I can keep going and going. All of this was when I was preteens. I was back and forth from Compton to Long Beach. I went to high school in Cerritos. Gahr High School. My parents weren't going to allow me to go to any high school in Compton or Paramount. They wanted me to have a better education. I didn't have issues going and coming from school. Like I said Cerritos is a suburb 15 minutes away from the north side of Long Beach. In high school all the activity was in my apartment buildings. Dice games, shootings, catching fades, robbing shit, some of everything.

I lost good homies back then. My nigga Scooby from Spook Town Compton Crip, T. Vill from Sex Money Murder Crip in the homie DeAngelo. It fucked me up mentally. It just increased by the time I got older and decided to take my oath. I didn't grow up in 151th St Original Block Piru. They gave me what I felt I needed.

Which means a sense of family. Ultimately, I was trying to fill a void. I was all in after that. Now the trials and tribulations are from the set. On West Side 1's Gang it is your own homies that'll treat you worse than an enemy.

Having issues and beef with your own homies is the worst. I've been in jail, riots, shootouts, setup and then some. But beefing with your homies? It can get tricky, my guy. It's deeper and then beefing with the enemy. Depending on the situation and variables involved, shit can be disappointing and heart breaking. If not, they probably really weren't homies anyway. Stand alone in Piru alone if you go to do it. As for the music industry, hey it's just our turn like it was for the Crips.

Rappers and people in general were riding that wave, entertainers were selling the Crip card back then and now. Just like the Pirus and Damus. For the individuals who are so concerned about rappers, celebrities and influential figures. Exploiting our culture just makes sure your backyard is cleaned first. Politics on your homies and members you know in the streets personally who are selling the P and riding the wave.

Being Piru or Damu is trendy right now on the mainstream level. Well, any and everywhere honestly. The out-of-town homies, love all. I look at out of town homies the same. We are all grown men and respect is respect. Now I'm not talking about West Coast gangs in other states that aren't official. Must have the right of passage. Whoever gave these out-of-state gangs the right to represent them is supposed to teach the right political structure. Homies need to listen; that's also an issue.

If the out-of-town homies are misguided, guide and teach them right. Old gang members from the 70s and 80s and then on to travel the country for various reasons in the flag went with them. Several of the members purposely misled out of-town homies for personal reasons. Several members put the blueprint down the right way like it was given to them. Some people out here are just bullies and being bully type shit towards out-of-town homies.

Some out-of-town homies are bullshit whether he/ she was taught right or wrong. It has so many variables but it's simple. Far as the companies selling death aren't that part of the gang culture? It's a part of life in general but isn't death part of the culture? When you see and hear rappers brag and promote death, violence, etc... Isn't that part of the culture? What is different because he/ she may be from the culture, participating in the lyrics or just witnessed these things?

I understand death is part of the culture and these companies are using this aspect to target us, especially our youth. But this culture was created by them. Created by White America. This has been set up by design from the streets to politics. We went along with it. Not all but a lot of us did. our own backyard and be more conscious of what we put out to the universe. These companies wouldn't be capable of achieving these types of goals. This goes for me as well indeed. Everything starts at home. A solid foundation starts in their household and with the Highest. Some tragic events that take place among our youth are inevitable.

But there's so much responsibility and accountability we need to rise to in order to give our children the best shot in life. Spending quality, teaching, and bonding is necessary. Like extremely. As for myself, I share with you my reasons for joining a gang already. Family love and teaching self-love is so vital, especially for our youth. Parents need to do better. Including myself. Tell the kids to represent your last name. Represent making your family a proud force on generational wealth. Chase your dreams in your own creativity.

Self-education is better than any education. Read more books and put your phone down. The millionaires and billionaires used and successful people read more than they watch TV. Use social media for business purposes only. Value your time and spend it wisely. If you don't want an average life, don't have average daily routines and habits. There is no limit. And love conquers all. The streets love no one, any person who says different is fantasizing.

Memory of My Brother Tai

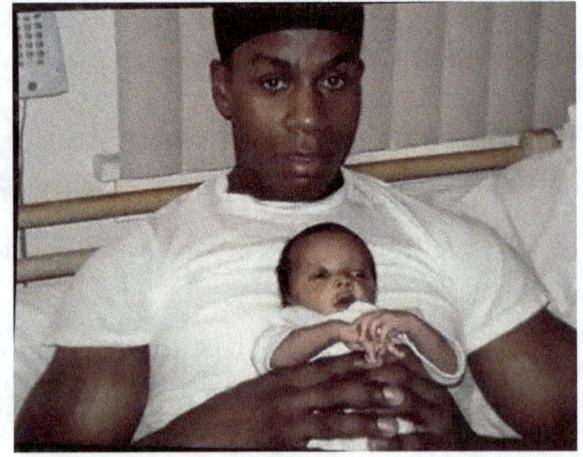

A loving father was coming from the grocery store with a young lady he was dealing with. Being a man, Tai takes the groceries to his apartment. Young lady was on her way inside and the young man decided to slap the young lady on her ass. Young lady informs Tai that was being a gentleman taking the groceries inside. When Tai was informed of the disrespect, Tai knocked the disrespectful young man out. The young lady goes inside, Tai not knowing the disrespectful young man he knocked out. Waiting for Tai to come back to his apartment. When Tai gets close to his door the disrespectful young man shoots Tai in the stomach. My brother passed away that day.... S.I.P Ta

Wasn't supposed to receive no more than 20 years, as he threw up his Set Sign in Court. They gave him 170 years before the pandemic; he gave back 50 years. Still fighting to give back more time "Lee Johnson"

During Father Duties

Brother was killed by his own homies after dropping his daughter off from school. S.I.P Lil Bg a reputable Fruit Town Brick City Brim from Newark, NJ

Representing A West Coast Set, New York Blood's Hated West Coast Blood's

The night of Jarvis Bradford's death. Julius and another person during that day were adamant about going with them. Countless went out to Harlem, New York to a club. Jarvis was on his way to be signed to "Block Royal" with "Akon". Celebrating that success on top of a person's birthday. Jarvis' life was cut short, he was representing a West Side South Central L.A Fruit Town Brims 36 St in" New York" back in those times east versus West was beyond thick. It was no different catching Crips on site. Jarvis was surrounded in the club by a set started in "New York"; Jarvis never once backed down. With pride and ego, they hated it. A few people that were around Jarvis admitted they felt something was going to happen yet they let Jarvis Walk to the car by himself. Not knowing he was being followed. Jarvis reached in his car by the time he turned around, and someone ended his life. Me and the person during that day were adamant about going, for one to support our brother and we didn't know the people he was around. We had a system when we went out anywhere. Never leave a homie or home girl by themselves when we stepped out. The bathroom, the bar, whatever. Whatever spot you were laying your head down someone needed to know. Too many wars were going on. His death sparked something big B.I.P J Vito

Talented brother, not just speaking, he is my brother from another mother Fruit Town Brick City Brims 232 he's really talented. We made any cake you wanted. We were in the feds together. Made birthday cards, pocketbooks, and designs. Yet unfortunately sometimes when we returned to the same conditions that led us in our condition of being plantations slavery prison, we don't see no hope. My brother is currently serving 17 years, and once again he was snitched on by a homie from his set again. As in this picture he was snitched on by another homie, friend day one served seven years.... Hollow Tip

My Rap His Reality

Was inspired to make it in the industry "Dead Wrong" rap about having a dream that he got shot twice in the head. Not long after he was shot twice in the head. The same night the gentlemen in the black baseball cap were shot in the eye by the same person.

Barefoot Pookie

Building with Co-Founder Westside Crip Barefoot Pookie....

Creating jobs and careers for when Bloods in Crips get out of prison. Blood told me out of his own mouth that Jersey was L.A second home.

Not Giving Up on My Son

I was seeing signs of my son the way he started dressing and a crowd he was having around. At that time my son "Lakazic" was 13 years old. My son being born and raised in Chicago; I was feeling helpless as if my words were not getting through to him. I understood what street life can be about but I didn't know or understand what gang life was about. I watch Julius developing growth, understanding not only the street but also the gang life, just arriving from an 11-year federal prison sentence turned around and starting talking to the youth who he holds dear in his heart. There was no doubt, I knew who I could contact to go talk to my current situation! Expressed to Julius how my son the Lakazic was dressing and standing. Julius asks me to send him the picture in like clockwork. He broke everything down. How my son's friends were definitely in a" Chicago Gang" . My son was on his way just because he changed his dress code. Seeing that's the first step, till this day my son remembers that conversation he and Julius had. Of course, you know it takes time for one to fully understand what was said to them. Overtime of showing love, talking, understanding, patience of course continued and with Julius staying in contact with Lakazic changes have come tremendously he graduated high school and he is now in the military. Passed four tests and was on his way to become a specialist in his field.

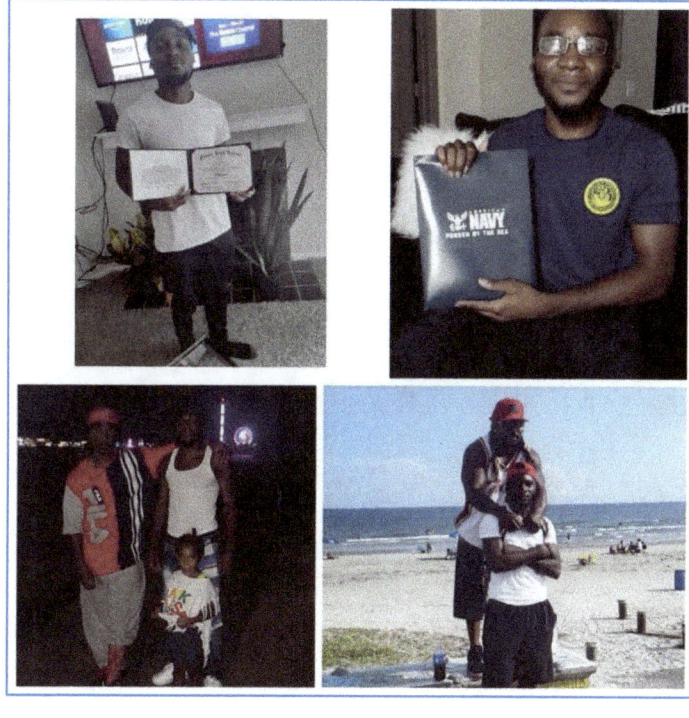

Retaliation

I'm in prison doing 40 years, and people say once a homie of mines from Fruit Town Brims 36th street was killed. It was said that I retaliated against a couple of people. I was supposed to have received five years, but somehow the courts railroad me with no evidence. I'm fighting to get back in court. From blowing trail, gang related. Since meeting Julius he's been the same solid individual. As we speak, he checks on my daughter and her mother without me asking. I never had to reach out to him, somehow, he got in contact with my daughter's mother since then he's been there, I remember the homie Kaoss told Julius it's a homie that doesn't have nobody on the outside. Julius asks for his information; he turns around and sends the homie damn near 100 pictures. And prison pictures are better than money in the sense. HBo A Reputable Fruit Town Brim 36th St.

Even With Life in Prison Still Has Hope

This brother has Life plus 60 years working on his appeal. Been locked up since January 2006. I sent him pictures in letters till this very day. He's working with important people from Newark, New Jersey named Michael Mincey to help redirect the youth from gang's non-affiliates to make better choices in decisions. I can also have him write if anyone needs assistance with having trouble at home day-to-day activity that goes on outside of home, school, friends etc.... Fruit Town Brick City Brim Kaoss

I Protected My Son

A young brother was going to meet some friends, at the time his son, a couple of months old was held in his arms. As he was walking up a flight of stairs greeted his friends. He was greeted from both sides with some bullets. While his son was in his arms. YG shields his son yet he dies from the gunshot wounds. His baby boy survived. He was upcoming artist B.I.P Yg YouTube channel Gunna Otep

Way Too Young

Young Lady on the left got locked up for a drive-by doing Crip killings once arrested in the county. Days later they found her body hanging from her jail cell. The young lady on the right was killed exactly a year after in a drive-by shooting. B.I.P Lady Break Bread & Kim

Never Turn Down Nothing

Young brother that was dedicated to his set Fruit Town Brims 36th St his life was taken by someone that claimed he loved the same set. His so-called homie killed him, he denied the fade and waited until he was high to do so. B.I.P Spazz a Reputable

Die For Her Respect

A mother of four and a wife was killed because she refused to be disrespected, and a man shot her in her face. She slapped the man that slapped her on her ass after the man was rejected. Every young lady and woman have the right to say no. Let me ask every young man, man how will you feel if someone put their hands on your sister, niece, mother, auntie etc....so why countless young men and men continued to disrespect any one of a simple rejection S.I.P Aiesha

A Line Up

The young brother on my left in the white shirt was killed by the same people that was said he committed a robbery with be careful who you call your bro, friend, homie, them titles are used to blind you from most people heeding agendas B.I.P Meech

So Called Friends

He was in the Federal Halfway house, went out with some friends. Ended up getting shot by some Crips instead of his friends taking him inside the hospital. They took him around the back of the hospital parking lot, threw his body on the ground and left him there. These were his friends. He was from Fruit Town Brims 36th St a reputable.... B.I.P Chuck T

Being Snitched on By da Same Person Put You On

I had a separate federal case but once Vincent Young aka No Good lived up to his name No Good he turned federal informant instead taking his life prison sentence like a man. Snitched on the whole state of New Jersey, even on correctional officers how we were getting weed brought in prison, cell phones got brought in prison and took a 14 to 15 years federal prison sentence. Got me tide into his situation I was facing the "Death Penalty in "Life Twice" behind Fruit Town Brims 36th St. No Good plea was life due to the fact for being responsible for bringing gang culture from L.A to the state of New Jersey. As well other homies B G never met, he snitched on him, so they can get out they own indictment cases. These the things nobody talks about I wonder why? For you kids the youth and young teens looking up to these rappers these entertainers any so-called Og live your life and listen to your parents or end up and get caught up in a situation like me.... B G is currently doing 35 years in federal prison Fruit Town Brim 36th St A Reputable

www.ingramcontent.com/pod-product-compliance
Lightning Source LLC
LaVergne TN
LVHW081556060526
838201LV00054B/1911